The Psychology of...

The Psychology of Abusive Relationships: How to Understand Your Abuser, Empower Yourself, and Take Your Life Back

By Pamela Kole

The Psychology of Abusive Relationships

The Psychology of Abusive Relationships

Table of Contents

The Psychology of Abusive Relationships: How to Understand Your Abuser, Empower Yourself, and Take Your Life Back 1
Table of Contents 3
Introduction 5
Chapter 1. A Common Story 9
Chapter 2. It's Never Who You Think 17
Chapter 3. The Abuse Dynamic 25
Chapter 4. Diagnosis of an Abuser 35
Chapter 5. Red Flags 53
Chapter 6. Control and Codependency 65
Chapter 7. Nancy's Story 75
Chapter 8. The Cycles of Abuse 83
Chapter 9: Emotional Manipulation Tactics 93
Chapter 10. Intervention and Therapy 121
Chapter 11: How to Leave Safely 133
Chapter 12: Lasting Effects 141
Chapter 13. Laura's Story 151
Conclusion 159
Summaries 161

The Psychology of Abusive Relationships

The Psychology of Abusive Relationships

Introduction

I had just gotten off the phone with Laura, who you'll read about later. She's a powerful, successful woman who spent quite a few months in an abusive relationship.

Throughout the call, she kept asking me, "How could this happen to me? I've seen friends through the same and I'm a confident woman. How could I have been so stupid?"

It's a question that everyone asks at some point. I explained to her about the cycle of abuse, the statistics, and many of the concepts you'll find in this book. They calmed some of her protests, but what remained was the overwhelming *shame* she felt that she was a victim of something so insidious.

That part takes time, and the more confident you typically view yourself, the bigger the failure you feel.

Abusive relationships don't just happen in movies or on the nightly news, they are happening in your neighborhood and backyard. However, you'd be doing victims a huge disservice if you just assumed they all started as malleable people pleasers with low self-esteem. They're some of the most confident, self-assured, and smart people I know.

How can that be?

It's important to understand the psychology and underpinnings of abuse: what the abuser's intentions are, even if they don't realize them, and how the victim is manipulated into acceptance and obedience. A unique dynamic is created that preys on all of the fears and hopes of the human psyche.

We all just want to be loved, and we want to avoid pain. Counterintuitively, that's what abusive relationships represent when we're in them. We're in them because we want to be happy and we don't want to hurt anymore. But what happens when our intuition is wrong and we feel like we're in an invisible prison with no options for escape?

The Psychology of Abusive Relationships

We start to believe what we're told, and our realities start to blur.

I want this book, **The Psychology of Abusive Relationships,** to be a guide for diagnosing your relationship through objective and insightful means, and gathering the knowledge to realize your inner strength and capacity for courage.

I write about my personal experiences, the experiences of other people, and psychological research studies that pin them all together in a confusing quilt of insecurity, manipulation, broken promises, and nefarious intentions. What remains is a startling view into what drives abusers and victims, and what you can do about it. You're much stronger than you think.

Come with me into the light.

Love,

Pamela

The Psychology of Abusive Relationships

The Psychology of Abusive Relationships

Chapter 1. A Common Story

Although I have many stories about myself, I decided to share ones of acquaintances and friends throughout this book because I felt it would be more powerful to recognize how similar these situations can turn out to be, even when they are from very different people in very different circumstances.

There are patterns that we must know how to look out for, and it doesn't matter who you are. People who are abused never fit into one specific mold.

Men and women are abused alike, and strong and "weak" people are abused alike. Everyone can fall prey to this insidious type of treatment because it can be gradual, and even subconscious. It can be the person you never thought would let anyone walk in front of them, or hold a door open for them.

These are all public personas, and you simply don't know what goes on behind closed doors. That's the scary part.

Without further ado, here is Esther's story in her own words:

Abusive relationship? I can't believe it. I always thought that was something that happened to other people. I even considered myself a semi-expert on them because I had done quite a bit more reading than other people, and had helped my friend escape an abusive relationship just the summer before.

How could it happen to someone like me? It was just for people like my best friend who had low self-esteem, or so I thought! After it was all over and I moved to begin a fresh start, I found myself falling in love again, and yet still couldn't shake the subconscious uneasiness at opening myself up and making myself vulnerable to someone else, especially when the last person I did it for hurt me so badly.

There are many aftereffects, to be sure.

The Psychology of Abusive Relationships

It all began a few months after I had gotten together with my now ex-boyfriend, Henry. Of course, the first few months have to be great, since they are the honeymoon period of any relationship. Everything is really sweet and rosy, and a mutual obsession causes anything negative to be overlooked. Racking my brain now, there may have been a couple of red flags at the time, but they didn't really start to show themselves until those first few months were up – until I was attached and semi-dependent.

At that point, Henry started to change into someone I didn't recognize at all. Where he was open and relaxed before, he became extremely jealous, controlling and possessive. He subtly began to tell me what I could do, what I could wear, and who I could see. I thought he was doing it for my own good.

Where he would ask for my opinions and solicit my feelings and emotions before, he would be dismissive and generally ignore what I tried to convey to him, even if I was hurt. He just wasn't the man I had fallen in love with, and yet he was able to characterize everything as being for my own good, and that he was trying to help me. Combine those feelings of guilt and stupidity with subtle manipulation tactics, and a few months after that honeymoon period was over, I felt like I was trapped in a prison, but it was all my own fault.

As a result of feeling so low about myself, I began to isolate myself from my friends and family, deciding that Henry was the one who was helping my miserable self, and I should be grateful that he was there. I wanted to show my gratitude by spending more time with him and waiting on him. Little did I realize that he was also spreading lies and rumors about me to our mutual friends. It was a sick cycle.

I felt grateful to be with him, but my everyday existence was incredibly dark and sick. There was a way that he made me feel like all the problems in the relationship were because of me. I took that attitude into every aspect of my life and my confidence took a huge dive.

I was a high performer at work before, but after Henry entered this latter phase, I became more of a wallflower, and no longer seemed to be on the fast track for promotions to management. I didn't feel like I deserved to be promoted, and was content to sink into the background and not let people discover that I had been an imposter the entire time, as Henry so elegantly phrased it for me.

I doubted everything I thought I was good at or even capable of. I felt lost, and yet despite it all, I wanted everything to work out with Henry because he seemed to be my shining hope of salvation. At least, that's what he always told me.

Was this love? Absolutely not from either side.

Henry got off on the power and control he had over me, and any semblance of love or affection he held for me was how good it felt to dominate someone. For me, I just felt so low, like I was drowning, and I would have gladly held onto anything that could offer me any type of refuge. Henry was that for me for almost a year.

This all culminated one night when I was so upset following an argument that I ran into the bathroom, opened my medicine cabinet. I emptied a bottle of painkillers into my mouth and washed them down with a mixture of mouth wash and water. I was just so frustrated and in pain, and I didn't see how things could improve or get better in the future. It felt like a dead end and I would just sink lower and lower.

The Psychology of Abusive Relationships

To his credit, Henry called 911 as soon as he saw me. He probably just didn't want that guilt on his conscience. I lied to the paramedics about why I took the drugs, and I didn't let on that it was related to Henry at all. I told them that I was stressed at work, with my family, and I was hit a weak moment where I couldn't contain myself.

While no action was taken against Henry that night, the hospital did assign me to a therapist during my stay, and it was there that things started to come to light and things started to change.

I had many conversations with my therapist, and they generally ended with him telling me that I was caught in the cycle of abuse. He told me that I couldn't hope to change Henry, and that he was the person in the wrong, not me. I was the victim. I had been abused.

Admittedly, it took a few sessions for me to realize the truth behind all of this, but once I did, I called my family and the few friends that I still spoke to, and two of them went with me the next day to collect my belongings from the apartment that Henry and I shared. I never went back or saw him again.

The Psychology of Abusive Relationships

The weeks that followed were terrible. How could I have let myself get into that position? How could I have missed all of the signs when I had helped my friend less than a year ago? How could I have been so naïve? I was quite hard on myself for how I had been seduced and manipulated.

How am I these days? I still sting slightly at the prospect of opening myself up, but it will get better as it has continued to. But it's a story that anyone can fall prey to, even if they're careful, even if they've helped a friend escape the same situation, and even if you appear to be a badass woman that doesn't put up with anything like I did.

Esther's story is scary for many reasons, but I want to emphasize that it's scariest of all to me because it shows that it can happen to anyone. And you know what?

There's nothing wrong with that. There's no shame in it. It doesn't say anything about how weak or naïve you are. Shed the shame and come with me into the light.

The Psychology of Abusive Relationships

The Psychology of Abusive Relationships

Chapter 2. It's Never Who You Think...

Nobody wants to be reduced to a statistic. In fact, no one thinks they will become that statistic in regards to abusive relationships, but that means that a good portion of us are only wrong. Not all of us are going to be able to avoid being involved with such a relationship, and it can be the people that you would never expect.

It always seems like something that will happen to someone else, until it lands on your doorstep. It won't seem real until then.

What's the big picture of abusive relationships? For one thing, they are extremely common. Statistically, someone in your family has been involved in one, and at least a few of your friends. In any given classroom, for example, at least a handful will be involved in one in their lives.

The Psychology of Abusive Relationships

They might not know to explicitly define their relationship as abusive, and indeed, these types of relationships are amazingly underreported, which makes you wonder about the real numbers.

As it is, there are various statistics to show just how prevalent domestic and partner abuse really is. Many of the studies only concern domestic abuse, while others only concern hard statistics and crimes. There are many types of abuse, to be sure, but the authorities tend to only report and get involved when there is violence or a fear of one's safety. As you well know, most abuse doesn't show up on the outside. Regardless, you will see an overall pattern emerge very quickly that will surprise you.

A study in the UK cited that one in every four women will be affected by domestic abuse in their lifetime, while one in six men will be affected. As I've mentioned, the true numbers are likely much higher because of people's shame and hesitation to report something that they believe would reflect poorly on them. Even so, domestic violence accounts for sixteen percent of all violent crime. The UK study went on to expand that on average, there are two women each week, and thirty men each year murdered as a result of involvement with domestic abuse.

The Psychology of Abusive Relationships

It is serious business where emotions run high and the consequences can mean life or death, depending on how you handle it. And it's not just a one-time traumatic experience that people happen to fall into because of a bad day. Domestic abuse has more repeat victims than any other crime reported, and additional UK studies have shown that there will be on average thirty-five instances of violence before the victim finally feels that they have to call the police to protect their life.

Thirty-five instances – imagine how much terror is present within the relationship at that point, and also how long of a time period it must have occurred over. They couldn't have happened in consecutive weeks because that would have been too much for the victim to bear. Suppose that they happened twice a month, because that would be enough time for the attacker to get back into the victim's good graces. Even at that pace, thirty-five instances would take almost one and a half years of terror and fear.

Some people realize the need to leave sooner rather than later, which contributes to domestic violence being the single most cited reason for becoming homeless and living on the streets.

Finally, the NCADV cites that there are twenty thousand calls to domestic violence hotlines every day of the year. That's over seven million per year. Staggering.

How did we get to this point as a society?

First, where do people feel they must resort to violence to solve their issues, and a lack of boundaries? Second, where men feel that is it acceptable (relatively) to physically impose their agenda, and will do so to the women they have relationships with?

As to the first point, it's something we'll get into more later in this book. There are many reasons, in fact, why people feel the need to resort to violence, and there are even more reasons why victims stay and don't leave as you might expect them to. From the outside as a logical bystander, there is simply no question as to the course of action to take, but when you're inside the situation personally, things look far different.

As to the second point, you don't need to look very far or hard to find cases of institutional sexism and domination by males over females.

The Psychology of Abusive Relationships

In ancient Greece, the city-state of Sparta was seen as extremely liberal and radical because women had the ability to be heads of households and hold public office.

In the United States, the Supreme Court of Mississippi upheld the right of a husband to "physically chastise his wife" in 1824. This same ruling was upheld by a North Carolina court in 1868, and it wasn't until 1871 that Alabama was the first state to restrict a husband's "right" to beat and discipline his wife.

Around the world, women have often been viewed as property, to the extent that it took American suffragette Susan B. Anthony years to campaign for women's voting rights, which was finally allowed in the United States in 1920.

In 2017, Russia's parliament voted to remove punishments for domestic violence against women.

Years of reinforcement as to acceptable treatment of our partners, especially women, contribute highly to the psychology of abuse. It makes it normalized and internalized, which by consequence makes it appear to be among the range of acceptable options.

Studies have shown that people encourage men to be sexual aggressors, with women to be the sexual gatekeepers. Parents socialize daughters to control sexual advances, and sons to create sexual activity.

Male aggression in all forms is more ingrained than we realize as a result of our social learning, and seeing that violence against women can be acceptable and normalized.

However, it would be an incredible disservice to ignore the other side of the equation. Domestic abuse affects both genders. It may not 100% equal, but if one out of every six men is affected, it's far more prevalent than you'd expect. Close to 900,000 men are domestic violence victims each year in the United States, which equals one instance of domestic violence about every thirty seconds. It's significant.

Separate studies by Strauss and Giordano show a pattern that might be startling. Strauss found that females are more likely than males to use psychological manipulation and aggression, which includes threats of physical abuse (though not necessarily the physical abuse itself). Similarly, Giodano found that females were more likely to threaten serious bodily harm by using weapons such as knives and guns.

It extended to actual physical abuse in other studies. Women were found to be more responsible for committing acts of domestic violence (11% to 25%), and in another study, 71% of the time, the physical violence instigator was the woman. In relationships where there was mutual violence and injury, men are injured more often (20% to 25%).

Does domestic abuse come as a result of self-defense for either gender? Do females tend to escalate situations to the point of violence, or are they pushed to the brink by males? Should we take into account the fact that women are inherently less of a physical threat most of the time? Is there a stereotyping bias at play here, where female abusers are more acceptable because it is seen as less of a physical threat?

For instance, does a man telling a woman to not touch him have the same impact as the same words coming from a woman's mouth? Likely not.

Overall, there is much data that can lead to many assumptions about domestic violence, but very few real conclusions. The only real conclusion we can draw is that it can crop up in relationships that you would never expect, and it's *complex*.

Chapter 3. The Abuse Dynamic

Even though the impact of the statistics can be shocking, it's still easy to dispel the thought that it is happening to you.

However, it can happen to anyone, and that's what I want to devote this chapter to. I want to talk about how the puzzle pieces fit together: why they are abusers, why you are being abused, and the unique dynamic that allows this to continue and occur in the first place.

I'll talk a little bit about the abuser, but I also want this chapter to focus on you and what happens to you during an abusive relationship.

Start with the abuser: they may think they love you, but it's almost never love. This is one of the things that victims always cling to, but it turns out to be a false belief.

By and large, what they love is the feeling of control and domination over you.

They love how you make them feel not because they enjoy you, but because they have extremely low self-esteem, and seek to belittle others to make themselves feel better. You become their punching bag to make them feel superior and intelligent, which is a momentary cure for their low self-esteem. Along with that comes a massive inferiority complex and need to be loved. All of these things can easily play out into abuse, because that partner becomes extremely selfish in wanting to make themselves feel good, avoid feeling bad and wrong, and will do it regardless of the consequences to the victim.

That's what being driven by insecurity can do.

Some abusers have strict traditional beliefs about the role of a man and woman, and that there is the right to discipline a woman who has stepped out of line. Some abusers are just malicious and like to see their victims suffer, and it can even become a game as to how much pain they can inflict on the victim. Some abusers have undiagnosed psychological disorders, which is something we'll cover later in this book. Some abusers learned a pattern of abuse from their family household while they were going up, and normalized that type of behavior. Some abusers have a self-loathing that they need to channel and express.

Some abusers are victims themselves and can only cope with it by lashing out at others.

And some abusers encompass all of the above. In some respects, it can almost make you feel bad for the abuser, since they may not realize the extent of their psychological baggage and the effect they have on others.

However, what's clear is that they don't have a normal conception of a healthy relationship. They may never have had one, and it's clear that they have a different standard than most if abuse is a part of the equation.

What's a healthy relationship? You could ask a hundred people and get a hundred different answers, but the answers will generally include themes of trust, love, intimacy, and support. If you ask an abusive partner, these aren't the answers that you will receive.

The Psychology of Abusive Relationships

If they are being honest, they feel that a relationship is there to make them feel better about themselves, cope with life, and outlet their frustrations. It's an entirely self-centered and selfish approach to relationships that occurs because they have no healthy coping mechanisms for themselves, so they must lash out at others. For example, if they are wrong about something, they usually blame the victim for causing the wrongdoing, instead of taking responsibility and accountability. If they have failed at something, they will find a way to insult the victim and make them feel low so they feel like less of a failure themselves.

Interestingly, the insecurity of most abusers comes in two parts. First, that they aren't worthy of love, and second, that they appear weak to the victim. Of course, they are weak, which is why they lash out, which also makes them less worthy of love. It's a sick, self-perpetuating cycle.

If that's the abuser in a nutshell, what is the relationship dynamic that is thus created?

The victim may have a healthier view of a relationship, which means they assume that that love and intimacy are the primary motivations. They will continually try to interpret the abuser's actions on that level, while the abuser, as we know, is driven by very different things. In other words, the victim tries to see the good and positive, but when they don't appear, the victim will blame themselves.

You can imagine that if the victim is constantly searching for a silver lining that won't be found, that their self-esteem and sense of self will come crashing down quickly. Instead of asking why their partner is treating them as such, they ask what they are doing to deserve such poor treatment from their partner that supposedly loves them. Of course, the abuser encourages this line of thought every step of the way. This causes the victim to withdraw from their family and friends, and seek the abuser for additional love.

It won't be about the partner's wrongdoing, it will be about what the victim has done to deserve the harsh words and abuse. The victim may not have started out as insecure, but that will be the biggest change they experience throughout the abusive relationship.

They will be told that they are wrong, they are at fault, and they are stupid on a daily basis, and that's impossible to completely deflect, especially if it comes from someone you think has your best interests at heart. You will start to feel that you are worthless as a person, and a burden in a relationship. You may begin to feel unlovable, and lucky that your partner stays with you even through your myriad shortcomings.

This is where the cycle continues: the abuser's insecurities are projected onto the victim, and the victim can't help but be affected because they are expecting love and support. The victim's self-esteem is destroyed, and then the victim seeks additional validation and approval from the abuser because they fear not being loved and being rejected.

However a victim saw themselves before the relationship, the daily wearing down of their self-esteem, supposedly in their best interests, will prove too much for just about anyone. You put up with the negative feelings and abuse you experience because you feel a need for love.

The positive aspects of your identity are gradually and systematically destroyed, and recast in negative lights. Eventually, you begin to believe what you hear about how pathetic you are. You're brainwashed, and your entire belief system has been subverted and replaced.

The Psychology of Abusive Relationships

Maybe you truly deserve this poor treatment, and maybe you're not happy with your abuser, but feel that anyone normal wouldn't want anything to do with you.

Abuse obliterates healthy self-esteem, and low self-esteem keeps people in abusive relationships.

You're not staying for the pain, of course. You're staying in the hopes that love and support will start to be the norm instead of the exception. You're staying because you feel that change is imminent (because they've told you as much), and you can see the positive aspects of the abuser. You're staying for the good days where you can actually feel love, not realizing that they come only a few times a month, and you walk on eggshells the rest of the days.

You stay because of memories of the honeymoon phase, and the hope that things will be like that once again. You stay because of the memory of a person who may or may not even exist. You either chase a ghost that doesn't exist, or chase the impossibility of them changing. Neither case has good odds for you.

The Psychology of Abusive Relationships

Even if you're aware that you are in an abusive relationship and want to leave, there are many hurdles to leaving.

The main hurdle is that they blame themselves for how they were treated, and feel incredible shame and embarrassment at the prospect of others learning of their weakness. They don't realize that there's not much they could have done to escape that abusive relationship because they are indeed victims, similar to victims of a car crash. They forget that basic human decency shouldn't depend on the context, and yet they blame themselves for not being able to control the entire situation.

What would people say if they found out, and what would they think about you? Public shame is important to some, but especially important to those that have had their self-esteem obliterated. It can be paralyzing. How might you feel if you blamed yourself for everything negative that occurred in the past year? You probably wouldn't want to show your face to anyone, further isolating yourself and lowering your self-esteem.

Other various hurdles to leaving are losing financial support, and a fear of bodily harm. Studies have seen that over 70% of domestic violence injuries and murders occur after the

The Psychology of Abusive Relationships

victim has left. If it feels safer to stay and not wake the dragon, then it's impossible to be motivated to escape it.

This is how anyone can fall into an abusive relationship. There are so many factors beyond the personality of the victim, and nothing is easy to see when you are with someone who you believe loves you. They lash out, you apologize. They pull away, you pull them back. They abuse, and you apologize.

The Psychology of Abusive Relationships

Chapter 4. Diagnosis of an Abuser

Though there is a small minority of abusers that have good intentions but bad habits or socialization, the vast majority of abusers have something *wrong* with them.

They aren't mentally healthy.

They don't process emotions in the same way as most, and they might not feel the same way as most. It's important to look this right in the eye. It is likely not just a case of misunderstanding or bouts of anger. It's likely that there is some sort of diagnosis for your abuser, and the more you know about it, the better you can deal with it.

In this chapter, I want to cover the following types of people:
- Psychopaths
- Narcissists

I'll also cover the following types of clinical personality disorders, which in many people can be undiagnosed for years:
- Antisocial personality disorder
- Borderline personality disorder
- Narcissistic personality disorder

Only through learning about the array of personalities that you could be dealing with can you understand how to protect yourself, and hopefully diffuse a portion of the abuse.

Psychopaths

Psychopaths are the first place to start.

A psychopath is frightening for many reasons and they are incredibly sharp and intelligent. They're calculating, capable of planning ahead, scheming, and concocting plans that leave most normal people confused.

Psychopaths understand exactly what they're doing to you, themselves, and their other relationships. They have complete self-awareness and know how their actions affect others, what their consequences are, and how they are manipulating you.

The Psychology of Abusive Relationships

The problem is they don't care. They just don't. They might tell you they do, and their words might draw you in time and time again – but look to their actions for a glimpse into their real intentions.

They want what they want, and that's all that matters to them. They have zero conscience and zero shame about accomplishing their goals at the expense of others.

Of course, they are smart, so they realize they need to keep up appearances, otherwise their ruses will no longer work. Social expectations and pressure, and their need for status to accomplish their goals is one of the few things that holds them back from being even more ruthless and devastating than they are. You'll soon begin to realize they possess many masks, all of which hide their true selfish selves. You fell for one of their masks and identities, but don't feel bad – everyone in their life has as well.

Imagine what you would do if you didn't care whom you hurt or how you accomplished your goals? It's a frightening thought experiment that is similar to asking, "What would you do if there were no laws to tell you what was right or wrong?"

Their selfishness rules the day and is their primary motivator. It gives them an impressive manipulative power because they are smart enough to make it appear as if they have your best interests at heart when they are really fulfilling their own goals. Their utter selfishness results in a total lack of empathy – even though they may understand how you are affected by their actions. You could call them callous to the extreme with a complete lack of remorse and shame.

They don't react emotionally in the way you might expect. Externally, they might show some remorse or rue, but internally they are continually scheming about how to extract what they want from every situation. They are pathological liars for this same reason – they have no emotional attachment and just want to accomplish their goal.

If someone were to die, a psychopath might show sadness externally because they know they should to conform to society, but they don't care one lick about the person's death unless it benefits or harms them in a tangible way.

Unsurprisingly, most serial killers can be characterized as psychopaths because their selfish desires override other people's right to live, and they show no remorse over what they've done — other than their remorse at being caught.

You mean as much as to them as does a screwdriver. You're valuable because you perform a function that pleases them, but once that function no longer matters, or you can no longer perform it, you become worthless to them. You are truly a walking, talking tool for them.

Narcissists

A narcissist is a person who is completely and overwhelmingly absorbed in themselves. The word comes from Narcissus who, in the Greek myth, fell in love with his reflection in a pond and never moved, thus starving to death.

They are the center of their own universe, and they carry that belief into how they interact with others. They expect others to also treat them as the centers of their universes and act accordingly.

This means that narcissists regard others not dissimilarly to how psychopaths do — as tools to be used to stroke their egos and confirm their own worldview. But there are some differences in what fuels this perspective.

The Psychology of Abusive Relationships

A psychopath uses people because they are missing the guilt and shame component in their brain. A narcissist uses people because behind their mask of egotism and self-importance lies an incredibly fragile sense of self that is tied up in external validation and can't handle any hint of criticism.

In other words, the narcissist goal is to boost their self-esteem and sense of confidence through whatever means possible – and that means controlling or using you in whatever way they can. They do feel occasional shame and guilt, but it's constantly overridden and vetoed by their need to confirm their own grandeur.

All their acts are a result of how poorly and negatively they feel about themselves, though they might not understand that on a conscious level.

In a sense, the narcissist is putting up such a sizable front that they never reveal their true self to others. But that's secondary to the narcissist protecting themselves.

They will take advantage of you, manipulate you, and show extreme arrogance – it's an attempt to prove to themselves and others that they are who they believe themselves to be. They are like bullies because they protect themselves through aggression and wielding power over others. If the narcissist must choose between averting a small threat to themselves and inflicting massive pain on you, they will choose the latter without a moment's hesitation.

Narcissists are the ultimate "Me first, me second, you never." To have any other expectation is to invite heartache. You will never be a priority or equal to them. You will never feel in control with them, or as if you matter. You will never feel as if they understand you because they simply don't care to. You will never win because narcissists have been defending themselves for years and are defense mechanism and rationalization experts.

Antisocial Personality Disorder

Antisocial personality disorder (ASPD) might be considered psychopathy to the highest extreme level. Where the psychopath might feel some degree of emotion, sympathy, or pity – even negative ones count – someone with ASPD doesn't feel any of that.

It's almost as though they have no concept of right and wrong, and they show zero regard for the feelings and rights of others. Indeed, ASPD is characterized by deceitfulness, compulsive lying, and manipulation to get what they want. You could describe them as callous, indifferent, and unsympathetic, but that doesn't go far enough to be truly diagnosed with ASPD.

This is a human being without a conscience. As such, they either ignore or fail to consider the consequences of their actions to other people. You might even consider them the ultimate hedonist because they pursue what gives them pleasure at any cost. Some people might appear arrogant as a cover for their insecurities and inadequacies, but the ASPD person differs here because they truly feel a sense of superiority to other people, and their priorities take precedence over anyone else's. If you give them exactly what they want when they want it, you can deal just fine with the ASPD. It's the only thing that matters to them, and that's what a partner or relationship also represents to them. They will use you to get what they want, and when they have no more use or benefit from you, they'll toss you to the side like a spent tube of toothpaste and find someone else who will satisfy their need.

What they want could be adoration, validation, or simply sex.

Here's what the American Psychiatric Association's Diagnostic & Statistical manual, more commonly known as the DSM, has to say about ASPD:

A pervasive pattern of disregard for and violation of the rights of others occurring since age 15, as indicated by three (or more) of the following:

1. *Failure to conform to social norms with respect to lawful behaviors as indicated by repeatedly performing acts that are grounds for arrest*
2. *Deceitfulness, as indicated by repeated lying, use of aliases, or conning others for personal profit or pleasure*
3. *Impulsivity or failure to plan ahead*
4. *Irritability and aggressiveness, as indicated by repeated physical fights or assaults*
5. *Reckless disregard for safety of self or others*
6. *Consistent irresponsibility, as indicated by repeated failure to sustain steady work or honor financial obligations*
7. *Lack of remorse, as indicated by being indifferent to or rationalizing having hurt, mistreated, or stolen from another*

These people are clearly dangerous on their own, so imagine the harm that can befall someone that enters a relationship with an ASPD. The definition of a healthy relationship is usually going to refer to a two-way road, with both partners benefiting. A relationship is never for the sole benefit of one party, yet that is exactly how the ASPD sees it.

Anything they do, it is for themselves, however they might dress it up or characterize it. They're smart, so they might be able to fool you, but their primary motivator will always be their own benefit and happiness. If it happens to benefit you on the way to benefiting them, that's a bonus, but not necessary. The ASPD can masquerade for quite a while as someone who does things for everyone's best interest, until you scrutinize why you never get your way or seem to be happy.

Borderline Personality Disorder

You can think of Borderline personality disorder (BPD) as someone who is incredibly unstable. There is no normal for them, and their moods oscillate between extreme happiness and devastating sadness. You can imagine how this plays out in any of their interpersonal relationships. They are the consummate *drama queen* other people will go out of their way to avoid, and yet, there are good times, as well, which draws people to them.

They simply can't control or regulate their emotions, which create relationships that are full of outbursts and anger.

When someone is extremely unstable emotionally, this means just about anything may set them off, and it's not always predictable or consistent. They are ticking time bombs, and you must be careful around them as there's no telling the reaction you will get. Something that was entirely acceptable and joke-worthy could be a damning insult the next day. Since they are subject to such mood swings, this makes them very impulsive and difficult to keep up with.

If someone has a tendency to take things out of perspective and let them affect their mood, the BPD lets small actions greatly affect and harm their self-esteem. As such, they approach relationships and even friendships from a place of fear and anger. They are afraid of being rejected, so they will often preemptively reject others through brandishing of anger and large outbursts.

With a lack of emotional regulation and impulsive tendencies may come episodes of suicidal behavior due to any imagined slights or fears coming true. Being in a relationship with a BPD is like being in a relationship with a powder keg, and you hold the matches even though you don't realize it. You can never feel safe or let your guard down because you don't know when the powder keg will go off.

Here's what the DSM has to say about Borderline Personality Disorder:

...Borderline personality disorder is diagnosed when there is a persistent pattern of unstable interpersonal relationships, mood and self-image, as well as distinct impulsive behaviour, beginning by early adulthood and present in a variety of contexts. These difficulties are indicated by five (or more) of the following:
1. *frantic efforts to avoid real or imagined abandonment.*
2. *a pattern of unstable and intense interpersonal relationships characterised by alternating between extremes of idealization and devaluation.*
3. *identity disturbance: markedly and persistently unstable self-image or sense of self.*
4. *impulsivity in at least two areas that are potentially self-damaging (e.g. spending,*

> sex, substance abuse, reckless driving, binge eating). This does not include suicidal or self-harming behaviour.
> 5. recurrent suicidal behaviour, gestures, or threats, or self-mutilating behaviour.
> 6. affective instability due to a marked reactivity of mood - intense feelings that can last from a few hours to a few days.
> 7. chronic feelings of emptiness.
> 8. inappropriate intense anger or difficulty controlling anger.
> 9. transient, stress-related paranoid ideas or severe dissociative symptoms.

Trying to love a BPD is next to impossible, because one day they might feel love, and the moment the clock strikes midnight they might feel incredible contempt and anger. You will keep getting pushed and pulled in dramatic fashion, and that can be exhausting if not dangerous. It also feeds the cycle of abuse which we will cover later, where you feel loved and you keep that memory close to you when you are pushed away in the hopes that it will return. It is addictive and can fuel a downward spiral.

You never know exactly where you stand with a BPD, and the spectrum can range from intense idealization to even more intense hatred and disgust.

Narcissistic Personality Disorder

We talked about narcissists earlier in this chapter, so what is the difference here?

Simple – where the narcissists we spoke about before were self-centered and selfish, it was all because they felt like they had to compensate for and hide a glaring shortcoming. To some degree, it was understandable why they would puff themselves up as such, and demand that people cater to them. They wanted to hide their own damage, so they projected it onto others.

The NPD is a bit different, however. The NPD isn't driven by insecurity. They have a grandiose sense of self that motivates all of their actions and the way they interact with others.

If the NPD believes an exaggerated sense of importance about themselves, then it's clear that they view others as inferior, stupid, and useful only to an extent. They have no equal, and they are doing people a favor by even engaging with them.

The Psychology of Abusive Relationships

They believe they were put on this earth to be worshipped, and aren't sure that anything is truly worth their time or effort. As such, when they see others in positions of success, they become jealous and petty, and lash out. Remember, the NPD isn't driven by insecurity, but they might have a rather fragile ego if they believe their sense of superiority is being threatened.

Think of how it would feel like to be in a relationship with someone that doesn't respect you or treat you well, and constantly makes you feel dumb. They're cocky and arrogant and can never put themselves into anyone else's shoes. They steamroll you in conversation and monopolize every topic. Everything turns into a story about them and they might barely acknowledge you.

People who have truly high self-esteem are typically humble, but the NPD rarely is. They'll do anything to feel the admiration and adoration that they seek. This can also simply come across as intensely overbearing and attention-seeking.

There are two parties in a relationship, three if you want to count the relationship itself. To a NPD, there is only one: themselves. You have to keep this in mind if you ever want to engage with a

NPD. They will only act to benefit themselves in some way, direct or indirect. Lower your expectations.

Here's what the DSM has to say about Narcissistic Personality Disorder:

A pervasive pattern of grandiosity (in fantasy or behavior), need for admiration, and lack of empathy, beginning by early adulthood and present in a variety of contexts, as indicated by five (or more) of the following:
(1) has a grandiose sense of self-importance (e.g., exaggerates achievements and talents, expects to be recognized as superior without commensurate achievements)
(2) is preoccupied with fantasies of unlimited success, power, brilliance, beauty, or ideal love
(3) believes that he or she is "special" and unique and can only be understood by, or should associate with, other special or high-status people (or institutions)
(4) requires excessive admiration
(5) has a sense of entitlement, i.e., unreasonable expectations of especially favorable treatment or automatic compliance with his or her expectations
(6) is interpersonally exploitative, i.e., takes advantage of others to achieve his or her own ends

(7) lacks empathy: is unwilling to recognize or identify with the feelings and needs of others
(8) is often envious of others or believes that others are envious of him or her
(9) shows arrogant, haughty behaviors or attitudes

Does the bringer of your abuse fall into any of these categories? It is not an exhaustive list, but it's very likely that they embody the traits of at least one of these categorizations, and it may give you a great deal of insight into what they want from you, and how you can either give it to them or beat them at their own game.

Remember the simple fact that these people are not like you and I. They are different in fundamental ways, some of which can pose an extreme danger to you. Be careful with whom you're dealing.

Chapter 5. Red Flags

We've established that it's difficult to catch yourself if you're in an abusive relationship, even if you think you've had direct experience, and even if you think you're the last person that would ever fall prey to something like this.

Perhaps if you've had direct experience, you might be familiar with the feelings and statements that would lead you into this trap. Otherwise, you need to be on the lookout for the red flags of abusive relationships, and that's what this chapter will focus on.

What's a red flag for an abusive relationship?

It's a sign to you that you are in danger. If what you're seeing has been happening to you for a long time, then you're already in very deep, and the abuse has been normalized to you. Your standards and boundaries have been changed, so it's all the more important to have some objective red flags that you can look at to realize where you are.

If what you see is relatively new and still shocking, and relatively unacceptable to you, then congratulations. You're not in a full-blown abusive relationship yet, or you will have an easier time drawing your boundaries. In either case, this is a good sign since it means that the abuser's behavior has not been normalized to you.

With that said, let's take a look at this thorough, yet not exhaustive, list of red flags that you're in an abusive relationship.

Red flag #1: Criticism and Insults

You feel like you are the subject of constant, embarrassing putdowns and insults. It doesn't matter what you're doing or what you've done, your partner never has a kind word for you. Anything that is kind is an insult in disguise, and nothing seems to ever please them.

As a result, you don't feel like you can do anything to make them happy, which makes you continue to try harder. This in turn repels them and annoys your partner, so it's a cycle where you can never win. Much of what your partner says is also extremely nitpicky and hyper-critical. They will talk about small things that they wouldn't care about in the company of their friends or family. They will be hypocritical just so they can ensure that they keep control and power over you.

They criticize and humiliate you to the point where you're embarrassed for your friends and family to see you being treated this way.

Red flag #2: Sarcasm

They say that within every joke is a half-truth, and that's exactly how abusers use humor. They'll say something under the guise of humor only for it to sting harder than a direct statement. It is as if they substitute a direct insult for a badly-hidden one.

They can communicate much more with a sarcastic statement or tone of voice than you might think, and it's done in such a way that is entirely designed to get a reaction or make a point.

You might also find that they are simply making too many jokes about you, which signals how they feel about you. It's one thing to talk about your flaws occasionally, but when they continually make jokes about them, it can get to be too much.

Red flag #3: Conditional love

This is where you'll hear statements such as "I love you, but…" or "If you don't change, I'm going to leave."

This takes your relationship hostage and immediately puts you on the defensive. It's an ultimatum that puts all of the power into your abuser's hands and forces you to take action, skipping every step in between. There may not have been any discussion prior to this, and there may not have even been any awareness. All you'll hear is that someone is placing conditions on their love and affection.

You're in a tight spot, and you'll probably feel compelled to change as much as possible to fit someone's requirements of you because you don't know what else to do.

This pattern continues until at a certain point, you may have changed so much that you barely recognize yourself.

Red flag #4: Feeling fear

Do you feel afraid of your partner most of the time? No?

Okay, what about occasionally? Is this fear about a physical assault, or is it about their anger?

Whatever the case, if you fear your partner in any aspect, it's a glaring red flag of an abusive relationship. Usually, fear comes about because we learn that we have something to fear – an exaggerated reaction or outburst, for example.

The fear begins slowly as avoidance. We avoid bringing up certain topics because we don't want to set our partner off, and we eventually have to walk on eggshells. Then we start avoiding other friends because our partner may become mad if we spend time away from them. We then start fearing the repercussions of our actions and that our partner might leave us.

The end result is that we fear so much, and avoid so much, that we become shadows of ourselves. Our confidence takes a dive and we generally don't feel like we have a voice or say in the relationship because we fear the strong negative reactions that we've seen in the past.

The Psychology of Abusive Relationships

Remember, it starts tiny. If you don't feel comfortable bringing up any topic with your partner, or your partner tends to have violent reactions, you just may be in an abusive relationship.

You don't know where the boundaries lie for this person and what they are truly capable of. That's terrifying. You know that they have a terrible temper. What could they do with it?

Could they hurt you and carry out their threats of hurting you? Could they destroy your belongings and punch holes in walls? Could they kill you, or someone else, if triggered sufficiently?

It all boils down to the question of whether you truly know the person you are with. In most cases, they might not show their dark side unless they are forced to.

Red flag #5: Isolation

This means that your partner prefers that you don't talk to your family and friends, and they isolate you from the world in general. They might do this by making threats when you spend time away from them to guilt-trip you, or they might do

The Psychology of Abusive Relationships

it more explicitly by forbidding you to spend time or talk with certain people.

Other ways they isolate are by texting and calling a lot when you're with other people.

It's almost always a one-way street. They can see whoever they want, and if you point out the obvious hypocrisy, they will say that they are keeping you isolated for your own good and safety.

This is usually fueled by massive insecurity, jealousy and possessiveness. We know that much of the time, the abuser's motivation is to use the victim to feel good about themselves and more superior. How can they do that if the victim isn't present? The abuser also knows that the victim might ask friends and family for advice regarding how they are treated, and they want to avoid the embarrassment and judgment that would come from the public.

These are things the abuser wants to avoid at all costs. They will result in a loss of power over the victim. Isolation is also how the victim begins to wear down and lose a sense of perspective and boundaries. Their world starts to be defined by only their abusive partner, with no one else to step in and deliver a word of caution.

Red flag #6: Rationalization

Without realizing it, you are making excuses for your partner's behavior and rationalizing it to be acceptable. If they lashed out at you, it's because of something you did and it was your fault.

If you're afraid and anxious, it's because you did something to make your partner act that way, that would make anyone act that way.

We do this most when we talk about our relationship to our friends and family. We'll explain a situation and edit it to make our partner less culpable, and then explain the circumstances which explain our partner's verbal and physical assaults.

Everything is always our fault. If this is you, then your abuser should be very proud. They have completely subverted your reality and sense of boundaries. They've re-defined how your very world functions and made themselves invincible and untouchable in your mind.

You are anxious to please them because you believe they are always right. You don't question them because you think that would make you appear stupid and ignorant. You don't call them jealous, angry, or possessive. You instead put the fault on yourself as someone who incites those types of reactions in others.

Red flag #7: Radical Personality Changes

It doesn't matter how confident you were before. Being in an abusive relationship will inevitably change your personality in a negative way because of the abuse and fear that you live through on a daily basis.

Your self-esteem drops like a rock. Your sense of self becomes severely distorted and warped. Your motivations change drastically until your abusive partner is one of the primary reasons for any of your actions. You become more withdrawn because you've been conditioned to believe that you are constantly stupid and wrong. You may have depression because of the general bleakness of your everyday existence and interactions with your partner.

You may have anxiety because you can never let your guard down. You may feel trapped because you have no one else to turn to since your partner has made you push away everyone in your life.

You may be suicidal because you just can't see things getting better.

These are small changes that occur over a longer period of time. You may not even realize that you're depressed or anxious – you might just think you're in a rut and overworked. However, where there's smoke, there's usually a fire. You must realize you aren't the person that you used to be, and there's a clear reason for that.

Red flag #8: Honeymoon Handcuffs

Without even realizing it, most of your days are generally quite bad and contentious, but you stay because you are seduced by how it was during the honeymoon phase. Good, romantic days are the tiny exception to the rule of abuse and insults. They are enough to keep you there indefinitely because it feels so good to get rewarded after so much suffering.

It's addicting. So much so that you completely overlook the fact that a good 75% of the time, you're unhappy, 20% of the time you're miserable, and the remaining 5% of the time can be characterized as normal and without tension.

Is that enough to sustain a relationship? Should we be holding out for someone that doesn't exist, or isn't likely to make a permanent comeback?

We're not fools to be seduced by this thought. After all, we did fall in love with someone. Yet, the way that they flash in and out of existence, only coming when they sense you are on the verge of either a breakdown or leaving, is extremely manipulative and malicious.

From their perspective, they don't want to try because they feel like they've got you in the palm of their hand, ready to do whatever their bidding is. Are they correct?

Chapter 6. Control and Codependency

Control and codependency.

What do they have to do with abusive relationships? They might not be the red flags that you would imagine, but they are dynamics that surface within abusive relationships at times without your realizing it.

They may sound similar to other aspects of toxic relationships, but it's because they generally prey on low self-esteem and depend on emotional manipulation.

There are many ways you can attack self-esteem and manipulate someone. The red flags mentioned earlier represent others, but controlling tendencies and developing codependency are major points in abusive relationships.

The Psychology of Abusive Relationships

Let's go through control and codependency separately to understand the roles they play.

Controlling people create their own world, write their own rules, and then proceed to suck you into it. You're not given a choice. It's their way or the highway, and if you have low self-esteem and think you are bound by love, it's an easy choice most of the time.

You follow and listen to them, and little by little, you are drawn into their world and their rules. It becomes your new version of normal, and it's only through a comparison of where you started and where you end up that you'll be able to see the difference. It might be too gradual otherwise.

There's a saying that to kill a frog, you simply put them into a pot of water on the stove and turn up the heat slowly. This is so the frog doesn't notice until he is boiling. We can see the various mechanisms at play through an example.

Suppose that your partner tells you that they don't like you spending time alone with the opposite sex.

The Psychology of Abusive Relationships

You might think that's an unacceptable boundary for you. When you bring it up to them and complain about it, they become defensive and suddenly turn into the victim, becoming offended and hurt.

You obviously feel bad, and regardless whether you want to or not, you cede their point for the time being just to make the pain and attacks stop. You didn't realize it at the time, because you were focused on something else, but your partner has just gotten their way even though you greatly disagreed with it.

That's where the control begins. You've just accepted their rules for the first time.

Next week, the same situation occurs. Your partner tells you they don't want you to go out with your opposite-sex friend alone, even though you made plans far in advance. When you refuse, they begin to apply guilt. If that doesn't work, they plan an outburst of anger to keep you in check, and wanting it all to stop, you give in again.

They don't think they are wrong, and when you broach the topic, you are attacked, even though you are the one who feels wronged. They make the issue about them and not about you. It makes no sense, but little by little, that's how control is exerted.

The next step is outright lying to keep you in check and keep you along the path that they want. If they're wrong, they'll lie about it, rationalize it away, or shift the blame to you. They'll tell you that your friends are toxic, insulted them, or cite a story where opposite-sex friends are always on the lookout for something sinister.

You might not agree, but if this relatively small thing is so important to your partner, then you might refrain from doing it just to respect them. They've gained more control, because where you would protest in the past, now you accept it without thinking.

It happens over a series of weeks or months, and it almost always involves things of seemingly no consequence. It's how the frog gets boiled alive.

What's happening is a persistent attack on your boundaries and way of thinking. There's no room for discussion. There is their worldview, and there are incorrect ones, including yours.

While it's not immediately apparent, this happens because your partner doesn't respect you the way you currently are. That's an important distinction. It means they want to change and mold you into what they want. They don't respect diversity of opinion, and don't like when they are challenged.

They want someone to fit neatly into their reality without them having to put forth any additional effort. It's also a reality where they are intelligent, always correct, and able to act however they want.

"I'm tired." "No, you're not."

"I don't want to see this movie." "Yes you do, you'll love it."

"I'm really upset." "You're fine. Let's just eat something."

"Let's go to that party." "No, you know you'll hate it. Let's eat pizza."

They actively work to define your reality. If others are fighting to define your reality, such as family and friends, you can also expect the abuser to interfere and drive a wedge between you and them.

The Psychology of Abusive Relationships

Codependency can be said to be the ultimate goal of controlling tendencies. In other words, a controlling, abusive partner would love to make their partner codependent.

What is codependency? It's when a relationship becomes extremely one-sided, with the abused partner relying on the other for all of their emotional and confidence needs. Their entire mood and happiness is dependent on that one person, and as a result they look to please them as much as possible. They allow that person to make all of the decisions, and shower them with adoration.

You can imagine the type of unhealthy dynamic that supreme power in one partner can create. With power comes responsibility, but the abusive partner isn't concerned with the wellbeing of their victim. They just want to use them to further please themselves.

This is the logical conclusion of a controlling relationship, and is also the epitome of enabling behavior.

Enabling behavior is where you actively help the abusive partner act badly. For instance, you make excuses for them, give them additional chances, or accept their excuses. Whatever the case, you don't want to disrupt the status quo, because no matter how bad it is, you know it can be worse.

You may not understand that this is a possible destination for you right now, but it's gradual and fueled by small actions that keep you in check, and small actions that lower your self-esteem so you don't look elsewhere. Some people are more prone to this type of behavior, but that doesn't mean it's acceptable to take advantage of it.

People prone to codependent (and controlling) behavior were typically raised being told that other people's feelings are more important than theirs, and they need to keep up appearances by not complaining or making a fuss. They were taught that appearances were the most important part, despite how unhappy you were under the surface.

However, realize that you're an adult now, and your duty and job in life is not to simply keep the peace for everyone else. You have basic rights, free will and to speak your mind as a human being, and you must assert them. No one else, not even your family or best friends, can do that for you on a consistent basis. And they shouldn't have to.

The Psychology of Abusive Relationships

Here are three steps to faring better in a controlling or codependent relationship, and to fare better in any of your relationships, period. They will give you the framework to simply understand the situation on an objective level and stand up for yourself.

First, you need to understand what you are entitled to as a person in any relationship.

You are not worth less than anyone else, and no one else should have greater power or say over you and your actions. You alone have the power to determine what you want and what you do. If anyone tries to take this from you, it is not normal, and something is wrong. This is yours, so fight for it. To this effect, you need to set boundaries for the type of treatment that you will and will not accept. Everyone's boundaries will be different, but there are some objective boundaries that should never be crossed – physical abuse, for example.

Second, your duty is not to swallow your pain and keep the peace.

You need to start to blame others. You may have committed a little bit of wrong, but that doesn't mean you are solely responsible for what occurs.

The Psychology of Abusive Relationships

Blame others for their part of what happens, and don't absorb their guilt. Don't make excuses for them, or rationalize why they hurt you. If you're hurt, you may be to blame, but so is someone else. This isn't to say that you should point fingers and blame others every time, but realize that it's never completely your responsibility or fault.

Finally, realize that you are dependent on external validation.

When you do that, you allow others to define you and what makes you happy. You give others the power of determining what you're worth. Of course, this can change in an instant, and where does that leave you?

Controlling and codependent relationships are difficult to see in the moment, so extra caution is necessary.

The Psychology of Abusive Relationships

Chapter 7. Nancy's Story

Remember Esther's story from the first chapter? It was a stunning look into a powerful woman that was taken down by a deadly combination of manipulation, abusive practices, and a cycle of destroyed self-esteem. It's not the first, nor will it be the last strong woman to be taken advantage of.

Esther, from the outside, appeared to be a very powerful and self-confident woman. How could she let this happen to herself? It's the simple psychology of abuse and abusive relationships. It isn't about her, and it wasn't about Henry. It was about the abuse and what that can do to a person's psyche and confidence.

I want to use this chapter to take a break from the analytical parts of the book and present another story of abuse, strength, and manipulation. Like

The Psychology of Abusive Relationships

Esther's story, it ends with victory, but is not without a lot of pain, and mental and emotional scars.

This next story is from a woman named Nancy, and it might seem a fair bit more frightening than Esther's story, but she still stayed far longer than anyone could expect. That's the power of the psychology of abuse. Here it is in her own words:

I was with James for about ten months, which is hard to believe. It can happen so quickly that you don't even realize it.

Before I met him, I was a top consultant in a top consulting firm. I felt like I was going places, and my latest promotion had brought me to a new city. In other words, I was no shrinking violet that couldn't stand up for myself.

In my new city, I met a new guy, and he quickly became the majority of my social circle there. It wasn't long until I felt that I needed to break up him with. I remember thinking at the time that it wasn't so unhealthy, but I was just fed up with his antics and immaturity.

So, I did it. I told him that we needed to talk and I said that things weren't working out, and we both needed to move on. I couldn't have predicted what followed next.

James threw a tantrum at first, and then he appeared to have a complete mental and emotional breakdown. He started to cry and scream, and begged for my love. He told me about how great of a fit he thought we were, and how worthless his life was if he was no longer with me. At one point, I excused myself to quickly use the toilet, and when I came back, he had taken a knife from the kitchen and was crying and holding it to his wrist.

I didn't know what to do except make the situation less tense, so I did the only thing I thought I could. I agreed to give him another chance, and he put the knife down. I knew in my heart that it was only going to get worse, but what could I do if he threatened to end his own life? It wasn't something I could live with, and I believed I would be able to find a calm way out sooner or later.

The next few months were hell. It was as if James knew that he had an advantage over me – threatening suicide. I was never going to take the chance that he was serious, so I would simply listen to him and keep giving him additional chances.

It eventually got to the point where I would do anything to please him and avoid outbursts, because they would come with an outstanding amount of guilt. How could I do that to him or anyone in general? I never once thought about how he could hold me hostage like that in a relationship that I wanted to leave. It was manipulation and abuse, and I didn't realize it until much later.

He once came into my office and made a scene because I was talking to a male coworker late at night regarding an assignment. He stormed right in, accused my coworker of interfering with our relationship, and flipped his desk over. I was nearly fired that day, and yet when I got home, I received a guilt trip so strong that I forgot all about that and wanted to make him feel better about my coworker, and reassure him that nothing was happening.

To ease his mind, he demanded to go through my phone contacts every night. I complied because I simply didn't want to deal with his fallout, and I was worn out. I had hit a point of fatigue where he could demand almost anything he wanted, and I would give in because I truly was tired of fighting.

Eventually, he started to hit me. My boundaries had so eroded at that point that I even stayed through that. I was in a new city, so I didn't have many friends, and my family was far away as well. What could I do?

My best friend from university eventually noticed that it was impossible to contact me, and that I seemed like a husk of the person that I once was. I was joyless, and she took notice. I mentioned a few of the things that James was doing to me and against me, and it was clear at that point that I was brainwashed. While they seemed run of the mill to me, they were absolutely horrifying to my best friend.

She lived about a three hour flight away, and that next week, without telling me, she flew over to my new city and took me out for a drink after work. It was at that point that I told her everything that had been happening, and I cried for hours on her shoulder. She was a wonderful listener, but didn't take me back to my apartment as I asked. She instead took me directly to the police station. I spent hours there detailing all of the threats of suicide, all of the manipulation, and going through all of my options.

It became clear that I had to take some sort of action myself, or else the system would be powerless. And so I did.

I went back to our apartment with two police officers. James was home and came out to ask what the problem was. He stepped cleanly into the role of innocent charmer that I vaguely remembered from when we first met. They just put handcuffs on him while I packed as quickly as I could through tears.

That ends the part of the story with James, but that wasn't the end of my battle with the abuse. Even though his presence was gone from my life, I still felt like he controlled me, and I still acted in ways to prevent offending him. My reality had been distorted so greatly that I didn't realize it.

I would think, "No, that's a male, I can't talk to him on the phone," or "I can't wear this, it's too much," or "I'm not good enough to pull that off." I felt like I wasn't good enough for anything, and the arbitrary boundaries that James had put on me were so heavily ingrained to the point of crippling me socially. I had no standard of how to act by my own free will anymore, and acting only to please myself and not be scrutinized by someone else.

Eventually my career recovered, and I moved back to where I was before, and where I was surrounded by friends. I found myself again with their help and have never been happier.

I'm comfortable telling my story to my friends and acquaintances now, and the reply is always the same, *"You?"* Yes, that's right, me. It can truly happen to anyone and I am living proof of that. I'm far past the shame of being a victim, and now I want to inform as many people as possible about this kind of abuse. We've all read about the statistics, but you never think you are going to become one yourself.

Trust your gut. Use your instincts. Ask for outside opinions. And love yourself.

Chapter 8. The Cycles of Abuse

At this point, it shouldn't be surprising that there are actually cycles of abuse that have been studied and documented to understand why, against all logic, people remain where they shouldn't.

That's because it's not based on logic. It's based purely on emotion and attachment, which can cause us to do outrageous things. It's important to keep that in mind when you read about the cycles of abuse. It may seem so clear to a bystander, or to only read about it, but it's quite a different story when you're deep in the situation and emotionally attached to someone that you don't want to believe wants to hurt you.

There are two main cycles we will talk about in this chapter. The first is the cycle of abuse, which has been studied for years. The second is the cycle of narcissistic abuse. You will find a few similarities and common threads

The Cycle of Abuse

This is the cycle that is most commonly seen in abusive relationships, and for illustration's sake, I'll use an example throughout.

It starts with abuse. This can be physical, or solely verbal, or both. The abusive partner lashes out in some way, and it's designed to make the point that they are right and you are wrong in some regard. It can be something tiny, but that doesn't matter, because the outburst won't be limited to that. The outburst will be broadly about how you are deficient as a person, and how stupid you might be.

For instance, if you suggested a movie to watch and you both hated the movie, that would be reason enough for an outburst. It would be centered around how they should have known that your taste was terrible, how they hate wasting money, and how angry they are at your choice (even if you wasn't your choice).

After the outburst, the abusive partner will feel some measure of guilt or remorse. They won't necessarily feel that they were wrong, or that you didn't deserve it, but they will feel regret over the fact that it might have been too much, and they won't be able to effectively manipulate you as much.

Much abuse is effective because it doesn't completely destroy boundaries. If that happened, it might be too much for us to stay for. They have to use just the right amount to make a point, but be able to apologize for it after. And that's just what they do next.

They apologize out of guilt, but they make excuses for what they've done. They didn't *mean* to berate you over the movie, it was just a long day and the movie was especially bad. They don't quite take responsibility for the outburst, but they say enough and talk around the subject enough so the victim feels better and exonerated to some degree. This allows the anger and hurt to subside on both sides. The victim feels in the clear about the movie, and the abuser feels that they haven't stepped too far over the line.

This allows for apologetic behavior as a means of making up for the outburst from the abuser. They treat the victim well and shower them with love and attention to make them forget about the

The Psychology of Abusive Relationships

outburst. You might even call this a renewed honeymoon phase from the effort that they are putting into the relationship.

They might act like nothing ever happened, and promise that nothing else will ever happen like that in the future. This part of the cycle is extremely important because this is what makes the victim stay. They enjoy it, of course, but it also gives hope that the abuser has the ability to change, and things will be better in the future. They feel great about the prognosis of the relationship and like a new person will emerge. Old patterns of the past will be dead and they can move forward with happiness and love.

Little do they realize that it's just appeasement and not actual change. The biggest flashing sign that it's appeasement is that it will only last for two to three weeks until something triggers the abuser again, and the abuse cycle starts over from the top. An outburst occurs, then regret and contrition, then apology and appeasement.

Once you understand the cycle, it's easier to understand how people can be sucked into situations they understand aren't good for them on a logical level.

When we are emotionally invested, we feel that the little details make the difference, but they never change the overall abuse.

Step one: "How could you choose this movie? I hate your taste and you wasted my money!"

Step two: "I'm sorry for screaming at you and pushing you. It's just that I was under a lot of stress and I really hated the movie. I couldn't believe you chose it, but I'm sorry. If your taste was a little better we'd have more fun most of the time."

Step three: "I'll never do it again. Let me make it up to you. Dinner at that fancy Italian place on me, then a ride in the park on horseback. Expect flowers tomorrow."

Step four: "I can't believe you chose this restaurant. Didn't we talk about your taste? Why can't you be more careful?"

The Narcissistic Abuse Cycle

This cycle shares quite a bit in common with the cycle of abuse. Namely, it is the tiny sliver of love and hope that seduces people into staying.

The Psychology of Abusive Relationships

The narcissistic abuse cycle has three general stages: idealize, devalue, then discard.

The idealize phase is just what it sounds like.

Abusers choose people who are high status or talented in some way because they believe they will reach their goal through them. They are idealizing these partners before even knowing them, and putting them on a pedestal because of the supposed value they will bring to their lives. They don't see their target as a person, just a fuzzy concept to use for their own status and progress.

Another way to put it is they see you as a notch on their belt, or a trophy to mount and check off their list. They want that status to transfer to them or speak well of them.

Despite their past experiences and sense that no one is a perfect panacea for their troubles, this is how they approach people. It's the only way they can ever engage with others – they see no other use for people.

The Devalue phase comes after the abuser has captured or charmed the target. Reality has set in and the abuser realizes that you are a person with flaws, you aren't perfect, and you probably can't do what they hoped you would. Most important, while you may have had some use to them, it's run out at this point. Your initial capital is all spent.

So they devalue you. First in their mind, then to your face.

They become unsatisfied and annoyed that they are wasting their time with you. They are only keeping you around until they find someone to replace you – someone that can take them to the next phase. They lash out at you, criticize you, insult you, and generally make you feel useless and unworthy.

They lose respect and attempt to create distance. The respect and adoration they once held quickly turns to contempt and disgust.

Tensions build, an incident or outburst occurs, a reconciliation and honeymoon period follows, then a temporary calm period arrives until tensions begin to build again. Rinse and repeat. It's a trap that many people fall prey to because of the promise of the honeymoon periods. The cycle encourages people to view a relationship through rose-colored lenses and remember only the euphoric honeymoon phases while ignoring the daily realities.

The Discard phase comes after the abuser has truly grown bored and tired of their partner.

Remember that abusers engage with people to use them for solely selfish reasons. This means your entire value to an abuser is based on what you can do for them. Once you can't do anything for them what use are you?

Did they ever love their partners? No.

Can they really cut things off so coldly? Yes.

No one truly means anything to them, and they feel about you as they might feel about a screwdriver – it serves a purpose. If a screwdriver breaks, you throw it away, and that's what they do to people.

They may toy with you for a while just because they enjoy your adoration and attention, or because they are just bored and entertaining themselves, but they have already made up their minds about you.

As you can see, these cycles of abuse can keep you in invisible prisons because of the mixture of pleasure and pain. You just don't know what to

The Psychology of Abusive Relationships

expect next, and you hope against hope that it's pleasure. If it's pain, then you still don't know if you can muster the willpower to leave.

The Psychology of Abusive Relationships

Chapter 9: Emotional Manipulation Tactics

Let's examine the tools in their powerful arsenal and how they use them against you. The abuser is many things, but stupid is not one of them. The tactics they use are intentional, whether conscious or subconscious, and are their way of keeping you in line and getting what they want.

Some of them may hit extremely close to home, and you may have heard some of what follows verbatim in the past. It can be scary and triggering.

But let's pull back the curtain and see exactly what they're trying to accomplish and how.

The Psychology of Abusive Relationships

1. Occasional approval.

Occasional approval is exactly what it sounds like. You can do the greatest things in the world for your partner, and they will only occasionally acknowledge it and show approval and affection.

It doesn't matter what you do. They have made a concentrated effort to show you only a certain amount of approval – a quota of sorts – to keep you under their power. They keep you under their thumb to keep you reaching for approval and feeling negatively about yourself.

Many psychological studies show that being positively reinforced on an inconsistent basis is addicting and keeps people coming back. It's the entire basis for **gambling** – if you won every time you pulled the lever on the slot machine, you would have no incentive to keep coming back and trying again. Instead, you stay glued to the machine without even knowing why.

Your partner knows this instinctively and thus doesn't reward your every positive action as they should. It keeps you searching for their approval, which is the equivalent of the jackpot at the slot machine. You may even become **obsessed** with their approval and it may consume you. This is not uncommon, and can drive you to anxiety. Ultimately it makes you afraid of being left by them, so you keep trying harder and harder to win their approval.

It's a cycle that doesn't end easily, and is designed to benefit only your partner and the amount of power they hold over you.

Example: You've cooked your partner dinner from scratch every night of the week. They only really thank, acknowledge, and praise you one of those nights. This makes you think the food on the other nights was inadequate, and so you try harder to cook better to again receive that praise you desire.

Consequence: You enjoy the attention they occasionally give you so much that it's like hitting an oasis in the desert. You may become obsessed with their approval and keep working toward it, creating an incredibly unbalanced relationship.

2. The disguised putdown.

This isn't a book about obvious red flags – there would be no point to that and you probably wouldn't need someone to tell you about them.

This is a book about the sneaky, underhanded, and plain dirty tricks that abusers use against you that you might not otherwise catch!

That's exactly what the disguised putdown is.

A normal putdown is, "Wow, you're really bad at that" to your face. A **disguised** putdown is couched under the pretense of another purpose, making a negative statement "acceptable."

It can be disguised as an innocent question, teaching, advice, helping, or offered solution, but the result is you are put down and insulted by a negative statement.

Your abuser knows that their hold on you depends on how superior they feel and how inferior you feel. They make it a point to demean and put you down at every chance possible to keep this power balance in their favor. Sometimes they are clever about it, such as with the disguised putdown.

This way, it makes it seem as if their **intentions** are positive and caring, despite the consequence of your feeling terrible about yourself. That may be how they justify it to themselves. Your abuser is a master of emotional manipulation and knows just what makes you tick – make no mistake, this is intentionally hurtful. And to make matters worse, it often comes from a place of condescension.

Example: Them: "Hey, you really need to work on your listening skills. You're such a terrible listener. Why don't you check out a book called _____, it's for people like you. You're welcome!"

Consequence: Even though the suggestion appears to be helpful and well-intentioned, you feel insulted and your self-esteem is lowered a notch. Maybe you ARE a bad listener. What else are you bad at? You can be sure they will point it out.

3. Gaslighting.

Unfortunately, gaslighting is a widely-practiced phenomenon that you may have even used from time to time.

Not to the extent that your abuser does, but it can be very easy to fall into gaslighting mode if you're not careful. But that doesn't make it right.

Gaslighting is when you bring an issue up to your abuser, but they immediately **invalidate it** and proclaim that the only problem is with you.

You can see how powerful this might be, as it allows the abuser to deflect all issues about their own actions and shift the focus to something irrelevant. They do briefly acknowledge it, but deflect it all the same.

It's also a strong refusal to accept responsibility in any form, which your abuser prefers because it means the responsibility will fall on you.

The Psychology of Abusive Relationships

When the focus of a problem is shifted back to you, the conversation branches off into all your shortcomings and this decreases your self-esteem. Most important, the focus is never on the abuser and their actions. You'll start to doubt yourself and conform to the new standards they have set for you.

This also conditions you to never show your displeasure or bring up issues you have with your abuser, because you know the result will be an argument, your feeling poorly about yourself, and your walking away with your tail between your legs. Of course, this keeps the power in your abuser's hand because they have just silenced you effectively without having to do anything.

Finally, gaslighting totally invalidates your concerns and can make you doubt whether they are even valid. This can drive you crazy with doubt and anxiety, and make you feel as if your abuser is the only one who will ever accept you.

Example:

You: "Why did you say that to my mother? That was so rude!"

Them: "What are you talking about? I was perfectly polite and you both just took it the wrong way. What's wrong with you two? Don't be so emotional. You need serious help and you need to learn how to talk to people."

Consequences: After they say that the issue is with you, the focus will be on you and any problems they choose to bring up, e.g., you're being emotional or otherwise in the wrong. This means that the original issue will not be addressed, and you are unjustly on the defensive... even when you are in the right.

4. Setting a smokescreen.

A smokescreen in normal terms is something that acts to conceal the true nature or intent of something else.

In an abuser's arsenal, a **smokescreen** is used to avoid and escape questions that hit too close to home.

Even if your abuser has ultimate power over you, it's likely that you've brought your concerns up to them before. After all, they care about you, right? They should want to remedy the situation and smooth matters over.

That's not their motivation, however.

They may want you to THINK that's what they want, but their end goal is always power and control over you. They know that having to truly answer many of the tough questions you might ask them about their feelings for you would destroy their power over you, so they simply avoid it.

They throw a smokescreen over it and use another issue as a diversion. Sometimes this might just be a topic change or deflection, which directs the original focus of a discussion to a tangent. If you really want to talk about the issue that's bothering you, you'll have to continually bring it up, and we all know it was a big obstacle to bring it up the first time.

A stronger smokescreen and diversion is bringing up a problem they have with you, so also be prepared to see that. This successfully allows the abuser to avoid the issue and continue their negative actions.

Example:

You: "Hey, why do you always ignore me when I say that I don't want to have sex?"

Them: "Sex? Last night, Conan was on and he was talking about that... he had a pretty funny joke about it. Besides, I don't complain when you forget to wash the dishes, now do I?

Consequence: This is a classic smokescreen. They barely address the issue of forcing sex, and the conversation is driven to another topic. Your concern goes unnoticed, and you just feel unheard and ultimately dismissed. The conversation trajectory then becomes their complaint about the dishes, conditioning you not to bring up your concerns for fear of being attacked back.

5. Snide side comments.

Snide side comments can add serious tinder to a flame. Even if your abuser has nothing but positive things to say at the moment, they might sneak in a few snide side comments to completely ruin the positive effect of whatever else they said.

A **snide side comment** undermines the positive content of a statement with a negative, and is disguised as a random thought, observation, musing, or simple wondering.

These comments wear on people when made as frequently as abusers do. Abusers fail to see the positive in praising you, and can't do so without making sure to remind you that you are low-value to them. And again, when you continually hear that you are low-value, it's impossible not to start believing it to some degree. Your **self-esteem will take a nosedive**.

Recall that abusers want to win, and they want power in a relationship. Keeping you in your place with a snide and rude side comment accomplishes just that, but it allows them to hide within positivity. They complimented you, they can't tell you the negative aspects as well? They can't tell it like it is?

It doesn't matter to the abuser how they feel superior to you – just that they do, and a side comment is an easy way to put you down.

Example: Them: "Great job singing that song! You're so great! Now if you could just hold some of those notes ..."

Consequence: Perhaps you pride yourself on your singing, but it doesn't matter that the abuser has said something positive. All you can focus on now is the negative comment they made at the end, poorly hidden as an observation. You start to doubt your singing skills, and your abuser has just lowered your self-esteem.

6. The guilt trip.

This is an emotionally manipulative tactic that you're probably familiar with.

Guilt works in the following way – someone wants you to do something and makes it seem as if **you owe them and are obligated to do it**. So you do it, despite not wanting to, and without an actual obligation.

Guilt can operate in many ways in an abusive relationship. If you bring up a concern, they will **play the victim** and guilt you into feeling bad that you said anything to hurt them. If they do something wrong, they will put the blame on you and make you feel guilty for (supposedly) committing a wrong.

If they want you to do something for them, they will make note of all the sacrifices they have made for you, the gestures they have made for you, and any miniscule compliment they have paid you. Your action should be in recognition and repayment of those things. This is ridiculous when you look at it from an outside perspective.

Yet all the same, **you cannot refuse**. You tell yourself they care about you so you should do things for them, even if you don't want to or hate to. Out of guilt and obligation, we normal humans do many things, and your abuser is keenly aware of that. They know you do care about them, and they easily take advantage of that … because that's what they can do when the balance of power in a relationship is incredibly skewed in their favor.

They are taking advantage of a perceived emotional debt in the relationship – a debt that they alone have created.

Clearly, this decreases your self-esteem and truly confuses your mind. You don't want to do this, but because you love them, you should. After all, isn't love sacrifice and being miserable sometimes? Guilt tripping forces you to act the way someone else wants you to.

Example: Them: "I can't believe that you aren't going to pick me up from the airport. I do things for you all the time. I bought you that scone. I fixed that closet door. What's wrong with you that you don't prioritize me?"

Consequence: This makes you feel worthless and ungrateful. By bringing up these unrelated things, your abuser forces you – through guilt – into doing something that you may not want to do or even have time to do. They make themselves your number one priority by making their love contingent upon your compliance.

7. Judgment and shame.

Judgment is something we are all afraid of, but it shouldn't be something that you're afraid of **within** your relationship. After all, isn't the reason this person is with you is because they accept your flaws and think you're a great person despite them? **A relationship is supposed to be almost judgment-free**. But, of course, an abusive relationship doesn't conform to basic standards or common sense.

Judgment in a relationship functions just as it does outside – if you say something to your abuser, they may deem it "stupid," "worthless," or "a waste of time" among other things. It makes you not want to open up to them or tell them anything you have done, for fear they will deem you stupid.

As with many of the tactics in this book, this is a power play that your abuser knows will lower your self-esteem. If they put down everything you like and do, it makes you less enthusiastic about doing those things and distances you from your own interests. And the effect is you **get used to** being persuaded (or dissuaded) by them and shifting your priorities based on their opinions and statements.

Their power over you grows every time they judge what you do and shame you for it, rightfully or not.

Judgment and shame are black and white, and you will be living according to that person's definition of right and wrong.

The shame and judgment aren't confined to the activity or thing itself – the judgement makes you feel personally unacceptable, inadequate, defective, and plain dumb. Your choices are your own, and any partner worth their salt should realize that and respect it and not make you feel worthless about your preferences and choices.

Example:

You: "I really like that girl's dress. It's pretty, isn't it?"

Them: "No it's very ugly and too revealing. She's probably a slut. Do you want to be a slut too by dressing that revealing?"

Consequence: Not only is this a repudiation of a casual comment you made, it's an insult to you. It uses your comment about something outside of you to criticize you personally by directly attacking your character. This shames you and makes you feel bad about yourself, no matter how untrue it is.

8. You missed the point.

This manipulative maneuver is particularly frustrating because it completely sidesteps what happened, and immediately invalidates your concerns.

Missing the point is as follows: your abuser will say something malicious or negative to you and you retaliate or become visibly upset.

Instead of rightfully and gracefully acknowledging your point and hurt feelings, your abuser blames you. It's your lack of understanding that's caused your emotional pain, your misinterpretation and not what your abuser said that is the problem.

Your abuser disclaims all responsibility for your emotional harm, and is essentially able to sidestep any culpability. The discussion then becomes about you, and your shortcomings in reading and interpreting your abuser rather than about your abuser's behavior toward you.

The Psychology of Abusive Relationships

Why can't you just listen better, not be so stupid, and understand better?

This is clearly not the issue at hand... and even if their intentions were pure, does that matter when harm is done? Your abuser will insist they didn't mean to hurt you, but that's often a lie. They know that hurting you keeps your inferiority complex alive and your self-esteem low.

Missing the point is reminiscent of **gaslighting**, except it uses misdirection to attack instead of a direct attack.

Example:

Them: "That was such a stupid thing you said to my boss, I can't believe you said it. I'm going to be so embarrassed by your thoughtlessness."

You: "Your boss laughed and told me he really liked me, what do you mean? I thought he really liked me."

Them: "Oh yeah…. he did. I just meant that you should be careful about what you say. Didn't you hear me? You missed the point. You're so sensitive."

Consequence: Your abuser directly insulted you and avoided the consequences of it by framing it as your issue. They get off scot-free, while you are left wondering whether you are indeed a bad listener, or too sensitive. It causes self-doubt and allows the abuser to say essentially whatever they want, whenever they want.

9. Words of affirmation.

If you haven't noticed by now, abusers take advantage of cycles of love and hate.

They do something to disparage you and make you hate them, but at the same time, there's something that makes you love them and want to stay with them. Often, this love is only misguided insecurity and low self-esteem.

Sometimes, it is a **one-way, non-mutual love** that the abuser creates with words of affirmation.

Words of affirmation are just what you want to hear from your significant other – that they love you, how important you are to them, they are sorry, and how they will never hurt you again. Only thing is – you never hear these things from them unless you are extremely upset and threatening to walk away. Or when they feel the need to exert their power over you in some way. It could be when you've reached your boiling point, but these words of affirmation are what your abuser knows will get you to stop being angry and stay.

Unfortunately, this probably isn't a true feeling of love or respect for you. It's just giving you what you want to hear to calm you down – **that's appeasement, not love**.

Abusers know how to turn the charm on – after all, they are master manipulators of people and know just what to say to make people like or believe them.

Even when you're angry, you are still vulnerable to these sweet words of affirmation, and they completely knock you off your guard so the abuser doesn't have to face any consequences. They make you vulnerable and sentimental, which weakens your resolve about whatever you are upset about.

Just remember, this isn't love. They love dominating and controlling you, not you.

Example:

You: "I've had it! I need to really think about this relationship. Give me some time."

The Psychology of Abusive Relationships

Them: "What are you talking about? I didn't mean any of that and I love you so much. How could you do this to me, no one will ever love you like I do!"

Consequence: There's a lot going on here. Your abuser completely rebuffs your concern and makes it about them as a victim. Your issue goes unnoticed and unaddressed. They break out the big guns with a phrase that you probably yearn to hear, which catches you off guard and makes you vulnerable to sentiment. Finally, it makes you ask if you are even worthy of their love.

10. Altered reality.

Each of our realities are relative based on our personal experiences and memories. You are completely entitled to your interpretation of that reality, and you alone are best equipped to talk about it.

But abusers cannot allow this to happen for two reasons.

First, it would expose all the devious tricks and tactics they use to maintain control over you. This would be devastating to them because you would see that they are intentionally manipulating you and attempting to gain control over you.

Second, it means that the abuser would have to live in the same reality as you, and that would objectively make them terrible people. They might not like seeing this about themselves.

So what do abusers do?

The Psychology of Abusive Relationships

Abusers alter your reality, which makes them appear more favorable to you. It's also a reality where *you* are the screw up, *you* are the person who doesn't understand them, and they are the best thing that will ever happen to you. It's scary if you step back and think about it, but that's the world your abuser prefers to live in.

They alter your reality by making you doubt yourself, denying what they said or did, remembering untrue stories, and invalidating your opinion and memories. It literally distorts your reality to the point where you don't know what's real or not, and you eventually bend to their reality. It breeds self-doubt and can even make you feel as if you're taking crazy pills – but then your abuser assures you that they are right and you are wrong, so what can you do?

Another variation of this is **selectively forgetting promises** and important things… basically, things and events that benefit you and are a hassle or chore to them.

Finally, the altered reality they create includes **direct lying**. Abusers will do anything to get the results they want, and they don't care if there are repercussions for anyone but themselves.

The Psychology of Abusive Relationships

This is all a tactic to get their way – at the expense of your sanity and reality.

Example:

You: "You promised to take me to the opera last week! You promised that we would have great seats and it would be an amazing night out."

Them: "No, I absolutely didn't. You must have misheard me. Are you crazy? Why would I promise that – you know I hate the opera. You completely misunderstood me, I was probably just making a joke. Get it together."

Consequence: You have just been completely dismissed and turned aside. Even though they probably did promise to take you to the opera, it doesn't matter now. That's not the issue – the issue is now your faulty memory, and that's where the discussion and argument will focus. Over time, you begin to question your memory and blindly start believing that your abuser is always correct. This is a dangerous slippery slope.

Chapter 10. Intervention and Therapy

At some point in your abusive relationship, you may reach an epiphany that you are suffering needlessly on a daily basis, yet you still want to see if you can salvage what's there.

It's the sunk cost fallacy, and we've all been there. We've been with someone for so long, and there is such history that we want to preserve, otherwise it feels like we wasted months or years of our lives.

We want to make it work with someone that might not be a great fit just because we've been with them for so long, and it seems so daunting to go out single again and find someone new.

Whatever the case, many victims decide that they want to actively try to stay in the relationship for the time being and fight the abuse in good conscience.

There are typically two methods people use to fight and address abusive relationships which are more than simply taking a stand. They are domestic abuse intervention programs and therapy, whether alone or together.

Intervention Programs

The most prevalent domestic abuse intervention program is undoubtedly the Duluth Model. It does have a few major issues, but it has widely been shown to improve outcomes and lower reoccurrence of domestic abuse.

The overarching theory of the Duluth Model can be seen as problematic, as it asserts batterers and abusers act out of a need to control their partners and relationships, specifically male abusers that act out as a result of a patriarchal society structure that subconsciously encourages the submissiveness of women. It' a feminist theory, but if we can ignore the dubious roots and origins, the Duluth Model is still the most effective program for behavioral change for a reason.

It's entirely possible to take a gender-neutral approach to the Duluth Model. As such, battering and abuse is only preventable when people's mental models are changed, and they participate in egalitarian relationships with their partners. This means that they fundamentally view their partners as equal, which also means there is little to zero ability to control them. Changing the need to control and have power is the main aim.

Treatment is focused on not just stopping the behavior, but changing the attitude and education regarding controlling tendencies, at the very least, to work nonviolently and non-manipulatively.

The main goals of the Duluth Model are the following:
- Remove the blame from the victim and make the offender accountable for the abuse.
- Create criminal and civil justice systems to hold offenders accountable and keep the victims safe.
- Use the experiences and voices from battered women to improve and create policies.
- Offer court-ordered educational groups for the offenders.
- Review current cases and policies.

This is accomplished through an intense, multi-pronged attack:

The Psychology of Abusive Relationships

- Mandatory arrest of domestic abuse suspects.
- Outreach and advocacy for victims.
- Aggressive prosecution and legal action.
- Mandatory rehabilitation programs.

In addition, the abusers are required to attend group therapy sessions that focus on the following eight themes:

- Respect
- Nonviolence
- Non-threatening behavior
- Trust and support
- Honesty and accountability
- Sexual respect
- Partnership
- Negotiation and fairness

During the therapy sessions, people are asked to examine their thoughts, attitudes and beliefs about relationships, power, and control. They examine their role in violence and why they tend to choose it, and other nefarious methods, to gain control and exert power. They discuss patterns of thought and attitudes in a more general sense as an attempt to educate and rehabilitate, as opposed to solve specific, personal problems. It's not like therapy. Therapy is intensely personal and focused. The Duluth Model is more of a boot camp to learn acceptable behaviors and attitudes.

These behaviors and attitudes are best summed up in the famous "Power and Control Wheel" and "Equality Wheel".

The Power and Control Wheel is a reference to unacceptable behaviors that are brought on by the need for power and control. They include: intimidation, coercion and threats, economic abuse and domination, using children as a weapon for guilt, minimizing and denying and blaming, isolating the victim from their support system, and emotional abuse.

The Equality Wheel is the wheel that lists all of the behaviors that people would ideally use in place of the corresponding behavior on the previous wheel. They include much of what is explicitly discussed in the therapy sessions: negotiation and fairness, non-threatening behavior, respect, trust and support, honesty and accountability, responsible parenting, shared responsibility, and economic partnership.

It seems clear that essentially programming the anger and disrespect out of someone should help reduce rates of domestic abuse. Where many people want to merely stop the symptoms, intervention programs like the Duluth Model attempt to eliminate the underlying cause of the behavior. If that doesn't happen, as a last resort, the abuser can realize that they are committing a crime and suffer negative consequences themselves.

It's important to realize that as significant as this type of intervention can be, you likely won't be able to do it alone. You might not even be able to do it if the abuser's family is on your side. You'll need to involve the police, the judicial system, and the legal system. Not only will they have the resources for education, they will be able to implement the real punishments and negative consequences that you wouldn't be able to. In other words, when you go through official channels and involve the authorities, you are able to dangle a sword over your abuser's head to keep them in line and continue their education. It's an unfortunate reality.

Therapy

Therapy is a controversial topic in the context of abusive relationships.

The Psychology of Abusive Relationships

Many studies and psychologists state that joint therapy as a couple is never the answer, because it characterizes the abuse as a relationship problem, when in reality it is due to one party's lack of boundaries or empathy. Couples counseling encourage a collaborative look into how each party has contributed to the problems, and that does not reflect what happens in an abusive relationship.

The decision to abuse is solely one party's fault, and the other party is the victim. There is no other interpretation.

Traditional couples counseling will focus on communication issues, misunderstandings, expectations, and entitlements. Does that sound like something that will address the root problem of one party punching the other partner in the face? If you focus on communication, for example, the therapist may even be inadvertently encouraging the abuse if the abuser feels more justified in their position and sense of "rightness."

Successful couples counseling depends on the ability of the partners to both take responsibility and be held accountable for their actions. As we know at this point, abusers are like Teflon. Nothing sticks to them and nothing is ever their responsibility. It's just how they operate, consciously or subconsciously. They depend on the fact that their victims will always feel responsible because it keeps them in control and with power.

What will happen if you engage in couples counseling with an abuser who isn't willing to let go of their own narrative? They'll try to manipulate the therapist to their side and place blame on the victim. They'll minimize the abuse and justify it with wild accusations. They'll outright lie and trigger the victim so they appear to be the calm, rational one.

If the therapist manages to see through their act, the abuser might just call them biased and refuse to see them further. They might even lash out at the victim for subjecting them to something that actually threatened their control and power.

And you have to consider the victim's side.

Will they feel safe essentially bad-mouthing their abuser right in front of them? They might not feel comfortable enough to speak honestly and portray the abuse accurately. What if the victim says too much and speaks too harshly about the abuser, and the abuser decides to take revenge back at home?

The Psychology of Abusive Relationships

Additional studies have found a few caveats that could allow for successful couples counseling. They focus on the ability of the victim to feel comfortable and hold the abuser accountable.

- The abusive partner works with a therapist on their own individually, or other types of work such as anger management classes.
- The ability of the therapist or victim to involve the authorities immediately, and the abuser to agree to this plan.
- A "no violence" and "no threats" pact.
- A list of mutually-agreed-upon instant dealbreakers, which would involve ending the relationship and immediate relocation as necessary.
- A list of topics to not discuss outside of sessions because they tend to trigger either party.
- An escape known to the victim and the therapist, that is unknown to the abuser.

However, in the vast majority of cases, until the abuser is able to be mentally stable enough to not lash out or abuse further, couples counseling is never recommended.

The Psychology of Abusive Relationships

Individual counseling has no such downsides with the right therapist.

They can allow the victim to see the true patterns of abuse they have been subjected to without filter or justification, and develop a plan for how to either leave or deal with it more effectively.

Victims of domestic abuse frequently struggle with their self-esteem, vulnerability and trust, anxiety and fear, and depression that can impact every aspect of their lives. Therapy can do wonders for these issues and help victims rebuild a sense of security, safety, and sense of self again.

Generally, therapy is one of the better options for dealing with emotional turmoil, because it forces you to process your feelings and change your mindset towards them.

Group therapy has been shown to especially benefit survivors of domestic abuse. It is through shared experiences with other group members that victims realize how unnatural their relationship is, and how common the manipulation tactics are. It also tends to provide a structure of much-needed social support for victims, which allows them to cope and bond over the familiar feelings of shame and guilt.

It can be difficult to expose yourself with such vulnerability in front of a group, but it is ultimately the exact type of catharsis some people need to become validated, and feel like they matter once again.

If you are lucky enough to get to the point where you (1) want to stay in the relationship, and (2) are dedicated enough to work on it proactively, you can see that you have options. Intervention strategies have been proven to work, and the best types are essentially re-education programs on human psychology and emotions. Therapy, on the other hand, can be a mixed bag since couples counseling is risky.

If you feel that you need to get out immediately, waste no time and read on.

The Psychology of Abusive Relationships

Chapter 11: How to Leave Safely

It's been quite a journey, and at some point, after all these realizations and stark looks at the reality of your situation... you just might be ready to leave your abusive relationship.

Of course, it's rarely as easy as just getting up and walking out. That's not easy for even healthy relationships. You're still on the fence because, as we've discussed, the devil you know is better than the devil you don't know.

In other words, you have been beaten into believing that you are lucky to be with your abuser, and no matter how bad your situation is now, it would be worse without them.

But that's living life by just getting by. Here are a set of realizations that you must truly believe and internalize to get to the point where you can feel okay leaving your toxic relationship.

Realize that:

- They won't stop hurting you.
- Change will never come in the way you want.
- They aren't who you think they are.
- They are in fact extremely malicious and manipulative.
- They are amazing liars, to the point where you don't realize they are manipulative.
- They are incapable of having a real, healthy relationship.
- You aren't the exception that will change them.
- Your relationship isn't an exception, and there are no special factors that make it acceptable.
- You have created a story for yourself where the behavior of both parties is perfectly acceptable and understandable and even rational.
- You deserve to be happy.

Why are these points so important to truly realize? Because they signal the end of the denial that has kept you in a toxic relationship.

The Psychology of Abusive Relationships

These are truths. It's your choice if you want to believe them, but it's a very important choice that can either signal a new beginning, or a life in jeopardy.

The next step to leaving your abusive relationship is to start examining the reasons you stay with them, positive and negative. You can think of this as a pros and cons list, but it's a little different.

For example, negative reasons that you stay with them include:

- Fear of rejection
- Learned dependency
- You're scared of not finding someone
- Pain avoidance
- You lack confidence
- You think you deserve them and their treatment
- Your finances are intertwined and you live together

Positive reasons might include:

- They make you feel good occasionally
- They have a fun dog
- They earn a stable income

See what's happening? Soon you also realize that the reasons you're staying with them are all negative and designed to avoid pain, as opposed to increasing your happiness. And if you really think about it, your negative list will be much, much longer than the positive list – because it's a relationship that is sustained by manipulating emotional highs, not happiness itself.

So how do you have that talk with your abuser?

First, don't wing it. Script it like a monologue ahead of time and rehearse it. Make sure you can think about it over a few days. Do this when you're separated from your abuser because you need to be emotionally stable and logical.

Second, what do you talk about? The key here: not much. You don't have to say much because if you do, given your history and proclivities, you will probably start to rationalize and negotiate with yourself to lessen the impact of what you're saying. So, don't say much. Keep it short and sweet and get to the point. Remember that "No" is a complete sentence and so is "We are breaking up."

It's not a discussion, you are *telling* them. The more you talk and try to explain your decision, the more opportunity there is for the PNM to sabotage your attempts and manipulate what you say to their favor. Do your best not to be interrupted and make sure you appear stern and decided.

If your abuser senses any indecision or weakness on your part, they will pounce on it immediately. And you never know, they might be able to convince you otherwise by appealing to your fears or simply acting so hurt that your guilt caves in.

You don't need to elaborate all at once, just say it's over for now – get your closure later or else it will just erupt into a huge argument.

Step three, when do you do it?

After you pack up, after you separate your belongings, and when you are at the point where you are set up in a way that you never have to see them again. We'll go over that part later.

This talk should be the absolute last part of the plan, not the first. After the talk, you should be immediately ready to avoid all contact with the PNM and thus avoid all attempts on their part to

The Psychology of Abusive Relationships

reengage and be manipulated back into contact and their good graces.

After all, they have apologized their way into your heart before, and there is a good chance they can do it again. So protect yourself here by planning ahead and making sure that you don't give them that opportunity.

In the same vein, don't tell them where you will be staying, where you will be living, or your plans for the near future.

Step four, make sure to set a time limit on the talk. You can do this by scheduling a car full of friends to come by and pick you up after 30 minutes, for example. This creates public accountability, and you can't very well tell your friends to just wait or go away. Make sure you aren't tempted to remain and be convinced and manipulated.

You're going to be facing a very lonely, tough road after you separate. It's going to be very tempting to go back, or even just send a text to see how they are doing.

This is the biggest mistake you can make, and it happens usually when you're alone.

The Psychology of Abusive Relationships

You need to recruit external help again so you can fill the hole in your heart immediately with friends, activities, hobbies, and family. Second thoughts strike when you're alone and lonely.

Don't be afraid to reach out to your old friends.

You will feel down on yourself and ashamed because of the situation you were in. But absolutely no one will shame you or think worse of you for the situation you were in because it wasn't your fault. People will realize that, and they will just be glad to have you back after being in your invisible prison for so long.

You will miss your abuser, and you will miss the stability and security you felt in the relationship, despite the poor treatment you received. But be aware that you're just missing having a partner, not THEM. That's a big distinction that can be difficult to see at first.

The Psychology of Abusive Relationships

The Psychology of Abusive Relationships

Chapter 12: Lasting Effects

What happens after you're able to leave the relationship, either willingly or unwillingly?

No matter what happens at the end, it's likely you still won't have closure or satisfaction that it's over. You'll realize that even though you've ended the worst part of the journey, you're about to embark on the second worst for many: the road to recovery and finding yourself again.

This chapter is about what happens after the relationship ends, and what you might find yourself having to deal with psychologically and emotionally. After all, if someone has been beaten either mentally or physically, there must always be a recovery period.

With physical scars, it's easier because almost everything will heal with time, and it's plain to see

The Psychology of Abusive Relationships

if you're healthy or not. You may have a scar, or several, but they fade over time, and you can even forget that you were injured.

However, with emotional and mental wounds, it's much more difficult. If you don't actively address them, they won't heal on their own. Instead, they'll grow and fester inside the longer you wait, and they'll manifest in ways that you won't understand. Time does not heal these wounds, and however much you want to immediately move on and tuck those memories away, you can't for your own good.

You opened your heart and trusted someone, and all they did was take advantage and stomp on it. You might not have realized it, but it fundamentally changed how you view the world and the people that inhabit it. There can be ripple effects that you probably don't realize until years later.

You might believe that the world isn't out to get you, that people are generally good-hearted, that you can control your own life, and that you are generally a good person of value and worth knowing.

The Psychology of Abusive Relationships

An abusive relationship can shatter all of these inherent beliefs because your abusive relationship has proven them false. If you don't believe that if you behave and treat others well, that you will reap the benefits of those inherent assumptions, then what motivation do you have to do anything? How can you control your own fate and happiness? Can you at all?

If you do everything right with the best of intentions only to be held hostage by an abusive partner, then life truly seems pointless to some degree, doesn't it? You can see how this would be a difficult mindset to rebuild from.

So, what happens after the relationship ends?

Aftereffect #1: You will likely be suspicious and distrusting of any member of the gender of your abuser. You might even cultivate a bitterness and hatred towards them, even if you yourself are a member. You just aren't sure that you can trust anyone, and you won't open yourself up to anyone. You also distrust your own assessment skills because of your past abusive relationship. You may have an overall discomfort with new people and especially with those that show romantic interest in you.

Aftereffect #2: You may have flashbacks, in the sense that you will suddenly be taken to a prior traumatic event from your abusive partner. It will feel like it just happened, and will be fresh and new in your memory. You will almost be able to taste and smell it. Your anxiety and alertness will be correspondingly high. You may have specific triggers that bring flashbacks on, or it just might be a general sense of anxiety that occasionally flares up into something more. These are traumatic memories.

Aftereffect #3: Similar to flashback triggers, you might have negative reactions to common, everyday things that you can't explain. The reason is these everyday things, occurrences, events, and locations remind you of your abuser, and when you think of your abuser, you immediately go into a dark, hurt place. Everything comes flooding back to you in a second, and you feel like you're still with your abuser.

Aftereffect #4: You may obsess and fixate over the relationship. Not over your partner, but over what you did and how, and when things unraveled. You constantly find instances in which to blame yourself, and then dissect what you could have done better. No one is saying that you need to immediately forgive and forget, but obsessing is

The Psychology of Abusive Relationships

the inability to let go and move on – to release yourself from the mental burden of thinking about the abuse.

Aftereffect #5: Some people may feel compelled to grab their newfound free will and essentially lose control. They feel that they've been under someone's thumb for so long, and been told what to do, that they want to experience the exact opposite. They can become unstable, compulsive, impulsive, and spontaneous to the point of danger. It seems like a way of taking back their power and free will, but unfortunately, it can be self-damaging at times. It also doesn't address the underlying feelings of resentment and hurt.

Aftereffect #6: You may be in a state of constant anxiety or sensitivity. The smallest thing can rile you up and alarm you, and cause you to panic. It's because the smallest things previously caused outbursts from your abusive partner, so you're accustomed to never feeling like you can be safe and let your guard down. Therefore, you don't. You're in constant fight or flight mode, and this is both mentally and physically exhausting. You're also extremely irritable, and prone to emotional outbursts as a result of being on edge.

Aftereffect #7: Very frequently, you will experience signs of posttraumatic stress disorder (PTSD), and the more specific posttraumatic relationship disorder (PTRD).

Aftereffect #7 is one that I want to dive into with more detail, because it is a serious condition that, just like abuse, people don't want to believe happens to them. But it does and can, so awareness and education is extremely important.

Posttraumatic Stress Disorder

Better known as PTSD – what does it actually mean, though? Usually you'll only hear this term in relation to soldiers that return from war because of the horrors they have seen.

PTSD can broadly apply to anyone that has experienced traumatic events. PTSD generally causes people to relive the event mentally, with memories surfacing unpredictably and causing crippling fear and anxiety. People with PTSD show "hyperarousal" and are suspicious of anything that is not immediately within their control. Being constantly on the guard for the next attack is exhausting.

The Psychology of Abusive Relationships

Technically, the type of PTSD that would apply to victims of abuse is called *complex* posttraumatic stress disorder. It pertains to a wider type of trauma and stress, over a longer period of time, as an abusive relationship would be.

A new category of PTSD has also risen to prominence, and it is called posttraumatic relationship syndrome (PTRS). It directly addresses the consequences of someone that has been subjected to domestic or emotional abuse.

The following symptoms characterize PTRS (courtesy of *The Neurotypical Site)*:

(1) Persistent re-experiencing of the event(s) in images, thoughts, recollections, daydreams, nightmares, and/or night terrors
(2) Extreme psychological distress (which may be accompanied by physiological reactivity) in the presence of the perpetrator or symbolic reminders of the perpetrator (e.g., uncontrollable shaking)
(3) Hyper vigilance (which may be the result of not feeling safe in the world)
(4) Sleep disturbances (insomnia)
(5) Persistent feelings of rage at the perpetrator
(6) Restlessness
(7) Difficulty concentrating

(8) Weight loss
(9) Mistrust and fear of intimate relationships (or a particular type of intimate relationship)
(10) Sexual dysfunction, especially for those who have been sexually abused
(11) Disruption in the victim's social support network, isolation

This leads to the all-important question: how do you deal and heal, even if you have PTRS?

The first step is undoubtedly making sure that you are 100% clear of the situation and safe from any future recurrences. This often means removing yourself physically and cutting off all contact. The main thrust here is to feel safe and be able to let your guard down slightly, and realize that you aren't subject to imminent attack anymore. When you feel safe, you also find stability. It's impossible to be stable if your world can be flipped in a split second.

For many, getting back into our daily routines and reconnecting with friends and family is a large part of feeling safe. What's more, feeling a sense of *normalcy* is also important, like you didn't get granted parole from your prison. You want to set up new routines and be able to set aside old ones that were dictated by your abuser. That's the first place where you can also exercise your power and free will.

Second, it's undoubted that you must begin to process the trauma you went through and what exactly happened. Don't feel a need to rush to this stage, as some people can take years to do this, and others can take weeks. Some people might be able to do this with their friends, and others might need professional help for years, depending on what happened.

It's important to start thinking about the fact that you were sucked into someone else's reality, and that everything you believed was simply not true. It was an elaborately designed ruse to keep you under control and insecure for their own purposes. Once you can accept that, then it's time to address the shame and self-blame that will inevitably occur, even though you are the victim of the situation.

Feel angry, feel sad, feel wretched, feel used. This is where you need to let all your emotions out in a catharsis instead of keeping them inside. Keeping them inside doesn't acknowledge them and keeps the truth from resonating within your heart and mind.

Third, you will need to reconnect with your life. The people, the work, the places, and find your place back within it. This is something that will not be without challenge, as your life and the world you left behind may not have changed too much, but you have. It may be a reverse culture shock to re-immerse yourself into normal life, so to speak, without inherent danger or abuse.

It may be difficult to remember how life was before abuse. You may not be able to trust people again. You may feel like your emotions need protecting. However, it's a process, and little by little, you will discover that people won't betray your trust when you slowly open back up to them.

There are many lasting effects from an abusive relationship, but beyond the rain lies the rainbow.

The Psychology of Abusive Relationships

Chapter 13. Laura's Story

Before I close out this book and send you along your way to heal, I wanted to impart one more story to you. Remember earlier in the book, we had the stories of Esther and Nancy, two strong, powerful women that you would never expect to be subjected to such abuse and pain.

Both of their stories were stories about sneaky, underhanded abuse and the effects that it can eventually have on someone. It wasn't about them as a victim or the perpetrators themselves, it was about what repeated exposure does to someone's confidence and sense of self. They can drive it so far down and below what you thought possible that they would be willing to stay through the abuse – and they'd even be grateful for it. That's always the scariest part, when you hear someone

The Psychology of Abusive Relationships

thinks they deserve it, and they are just happy to not be alone.

This last story comes to you from Laura. Here it is in her words:

My abusive relationship was my first. I got married right when I turned eighteen. I think it must have been some sort of reaction to my parents and I wanted to rebel against them. I married the boy I dated for about six months in high school and immediately moved to another region with him. He was four years older, and I honestly didn't know him that well.

Chalk it up to teenage bravado and stupidity. I thought I was going to beat the odds and my young marriage was going to end up just fine. Admittedly, there were some days where I did indeed feel happy, but looking back, it was because I lacked any type of real standard for how I should have been treated in a relationship. I met Jack when I was seventeen, and he was my first boyfriend as well. I had no experience and no idea of what to expect. I knew my expectations weren't going to match a Disney movie's happy ending, but I expected some degree of happiness.

The Psychology of Abusive Relationships

That wasn't what I got. Jack was very controlling from the moment we started dating. He instantly began to alienate my friends with odd behavior, and generally making them feel uncomfortable and unwelcome. Remember, I had no prior real experience with the opposite sex, so I didn't truly see that something was wrong until much later. I thought he was just asserting his right and privilege as my boyfriend, and that I was supposed to be entirely devoted to him and ignore all other people.

I want to emphasize the fact that it all seemed normal to me, and eventually the worse it got, that also seemed normal to me. I just didn't know, and that's a very dangerous place to be coming from. I didn't know, and I also didn't ask anyone because I was afraid of what they might tell me to burst my little happy bubble.

Jack was eventually so controlling to the point where the only people I was allowed to speak to were him, his family, and a couple of his female friends. I may not have had standards, but that finally didn't sit right with me, and I started to ask why I couldn't keep in touch with my family or my own friends anymore. He blew up and said that it was a matter of respect, and that I should respect his wishes, and keep myself free of bad influences like my friends. Again, I had no standard for treatment, so I just nodded my head and filed the complaint away for another day.

In hindsight, he brandished his anger as a weapon against me, to keep me quiet and from speaking up about my concerns.

Jack also didn't permit me to get any type of job. Instead we both relied on his close-to-minimum wage job and it showed in our lifestyle. We were always struggling for money, despite me continually asking to help out and get at least a part-time job. In hindsight, this was to keep me dependent upon him, so he could always claim the moral high ground for control and decisions because he made the money, so he would have the say on how to spend it.

It's scary the lengths he went to assert his control.

One fortuitous weekend, a couple of my female high school friends were coming into town to visit another mutual friend of ours. Naturally, I was invited out as a sort of small reunion. I ran this plan past Jack and he made it clear that he didn't want me going, but he was also headed out the door and couldn't give me a full argument to sway me to his side, so I ended up meeting them for dinner and drinks.

With four women at the table, you can imagine that one of the first topics brought up was our significant others. They all took turns gabbing about the men they'd met and dated over the past years, but I kept quiet. I was prodded constantly by one of my friends until I decided that I had some questions I wanted to ask them.

What degree of controlling is normal?
What amount of deference should I be giving a man?
Was Jack normal?
Was I in a bad relationship?
Was it my fault?
Did I deserve to be treated like this?

I would ask a question that gave away how I was treated, then argue with them and rationalize the situation I found myself in. This pattern repeated itself a few times until one of my friends simply said, "Look, whether you realize it or not, you are in an abusive relationship. All we can do is tell you that this isn't normal and this isn't love, and you can do with that what you want."

The Psychology of Abusive Relationships

I went home feeling dejected, and like they didn't understand the intricacies of my relationship with Jack. I obviously didn't have anyone else to talk to, so I brought the issue up with Jack when I got home.

I asked him why I felt terrible in our relationship, and why he tried to dictate so many aspects of my life. I thought it was an innocent question, and I tried to phrase it as meekly as possible, but it didn't seem to matter.

Jack flew into what can only be described as a fit of rage. He pushed me against the wall with his hands around my neck. He was suffocating me, and he only let go of my throat when I started to black out and collapse onto the floor. His explanation as I sat in a crumpled pile on the ground? That it was insulting that he tried so hard to support and take care of me, and I repaid him by asking ridiculous questions and doubting his motives.

That was the first time he laid his hands on me and it was the last. That was finally the point where I decided things were not as they seemed, and I needed to remove myself from the situation.

The Psychology of Abusive Relationships

My big mistake was to attempt to engage in a discussion with him about breaking up, as opposed to distancing myself first and then dealing with the fallout. You see, the entire problem of that relationship with Jack was that he could say things that threw me off completely and make me forget what I wanted.

If he wasn't guilt tripping me, he manipulated and persuaded me otherwise, threatened me in subtle ways, insulted and mocked me, pointed out how low my confidence was, and how he was the best thing to ever happen to me.

I would have these discussions with him almost weekly until I decided that a discussion didn't need to happen. I had made up my mind, and when he went to work in the morning, I called a cousin who lived nearby to come with his car. I loaded everything into it and left Jack a note on the kitchen table.

The note didn't say where I'd be, or why I'd left. He didn't need to know where I would be, and he should have known at that point why I would leave. The note just said "I'm sorry" because I truly was, and I wasn't yet convinced that I was doing the right thing.

It took another few weeks, and countless talks with my friends and family, for me to realize that I was a prisoner of abuse, and I deserved more than that. Perhaps I should have drawn the line at being choked, and I repeatedly berated myself for taking Jack's bait and staying even longer. I rarely do anymore because I realize I was a victim, just like how some are victims of car accidents. It wasn't my fault and there wasn't much I could have done to change the situation.

I'm comfortable with that now, and I like to think that I have very few emotional scars at this point. I'm guarded when it comes to new people, and I rely on my support network quite a bit to help me filter them. I may trust my gut and instincts less than other people. I may occasionally struggle with low self-esteem. But I got out alive. I can't take that for granted.

Conclusion

You've read some of my journey. You've also seen Laura's, Esther's, and Nancy's journeys.

They aren't the type of people doomed to become a statistic, and neither are you. So what happened?

The staggering combination of emotions, attachment, and manipulation happened. They forced you to construct your own invisible prison from which you couldn't escape for the life of you.

It's time to break free and find your power again. Picture the best, ideal version of yourself – they still exist. You can get there again. But the first step is taking the giant leap of faith away from your abuser.

Love,
Pamela

The Psychology of Abusive Relationships

The Psychology of Abusive Relationships

Summaries

Chapter 1. A Common Story

Abusive relationships are such a common story that the concepts of love, abuse, manipulation, and happiness are mentally mutated and twisted to fit your needs.

Chapter 2. It's Never Who You Think...

The statistics on abuse are shocking, and that includes information on both genders as victims. Socialized behavior and attitudes towards relationships and women are partially to blame for the prevalence.

Chapter 3. The Abuse Dynamic

Just because you are a victim doesn't mean you are weak. The abuser creates a very specific type

The Psychology of Abusive Relationships

of relationship dynamic that causes your self-esteem to drop while their ego and control grows.

Chapter 4. Diagnosis of an Abuser

Abusers are not like you. They can be narcissists, psychopaths, or suffer from a clinical disorder such as antisocial personality disorder, borderline personality disorder, or narcissistic personality disorder.

Chapter 5. Red Flags

Red flags are small cues that we are not as happy as we should be, and they include fear, isolation, general unhappiness, rationalization of bad behavior, and an overall depressed state.

Chapter 6. Control and Codependency

Codependency can be said to be the ultimate end goal of a controlling relationship. Your abuser wants you to rely on them, which increases their power and control.

Chapter 7. Nancy's Story

Sometimes we are consciously manipulated, but we can't do anything about it. Nancy's ex told her he would kill himself if she left. What can one do in the heat of the moment?

Chapter 8. The Cycles of Abuse

The cycles are abuse are what bind us to our abusers. They are highlighted and brought together by the honeymoon phase – which was either a false representation of the abuser, or something that never was at all.

Chapter 9: Emotional Manipulation Tactics

There are many subtle ways your abuser can manipulate your emotions and bend you to their preferences and commands. Among them are gaslighting, guilt trips, the silent treatment, and shaming you.

Chapter 10. Intervention and Therapy

The most prevalent intervention treatment is called the Duluth Model and works by changing ingrained beliefs and attitudes towards relationship management. Solo therapy is recommended, but not couples therapy.

Chapter 11: How to Leave Safely

The Psychology of Abusive Relationships

To leave safely, telling (not discussing) them of your plans to leave should be the last step. Everything else should be ready, because if not, there is a high likelihood of intense manipulation to stay.

Chapter 12: Lasting Effects

You will have scars for a while. You may find it difficult to trust or become vulnerable. You may even have a distinct type of PTSD surrounding other people and intimacy.

Chapter 13. Laura's Story

Laura's story is an eye-opening example into the standards we set for ourselves and how we allow ourselves to be treated if we don't know any better.

Made in the USA
San Bernardino, CA
01 May 2017